I0489397

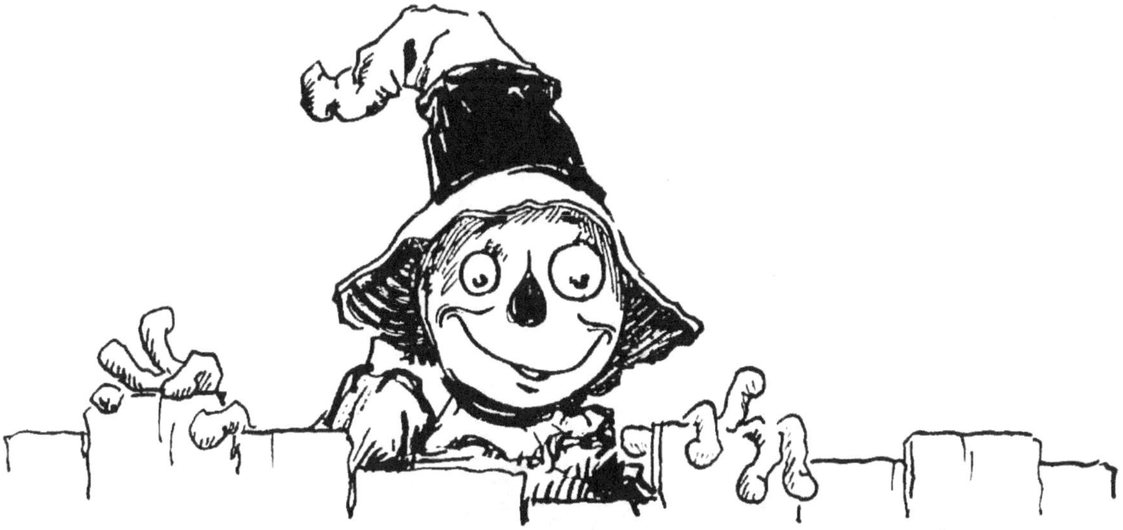

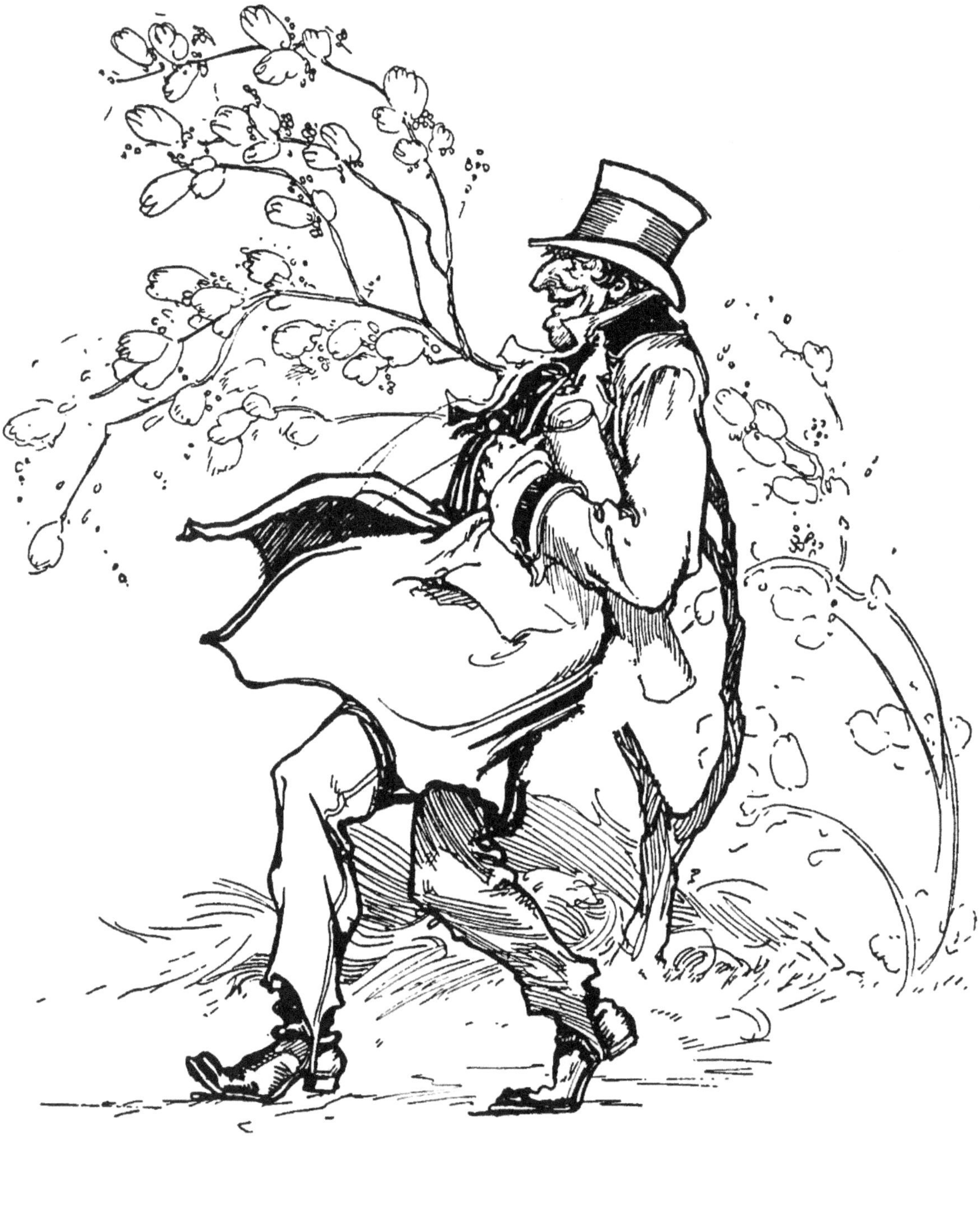

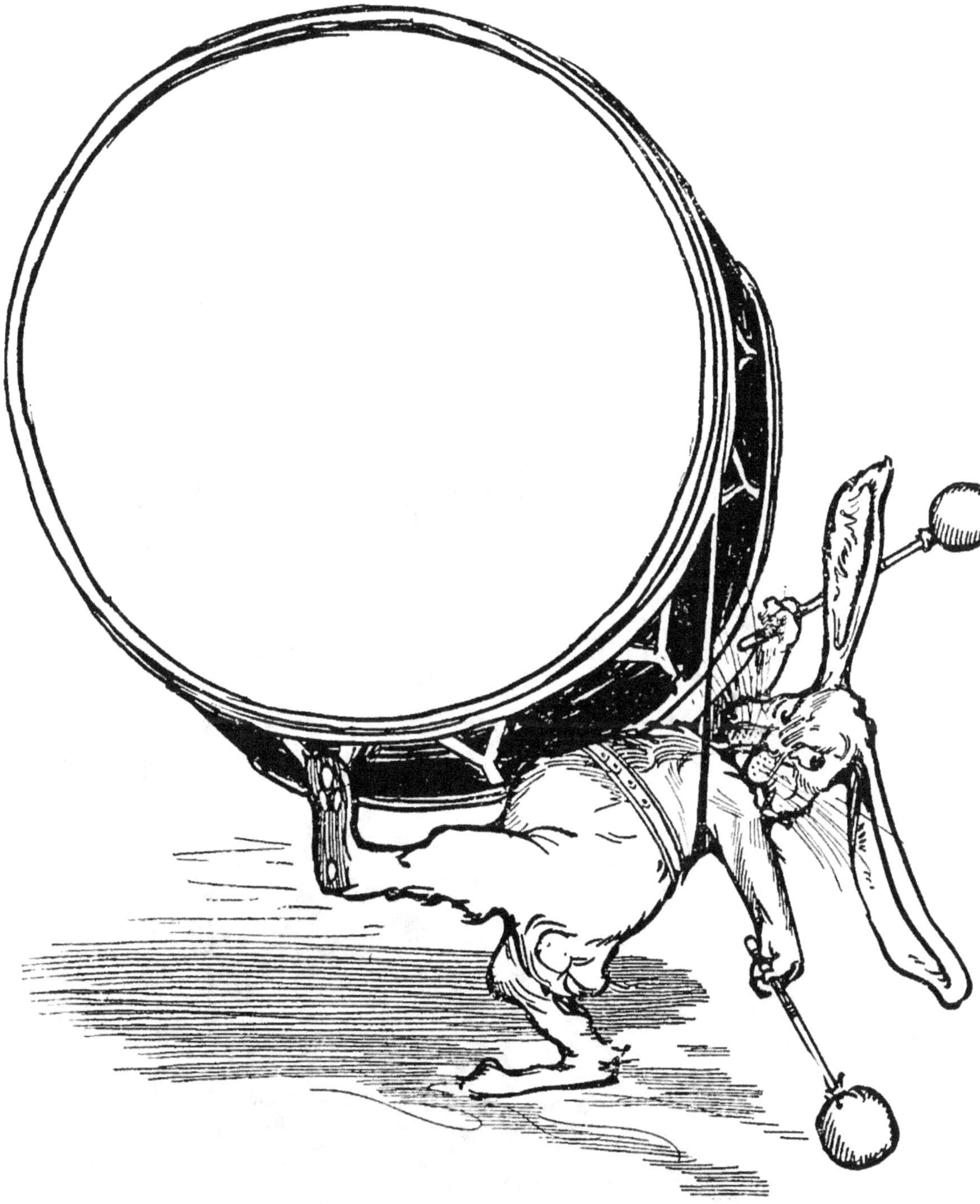

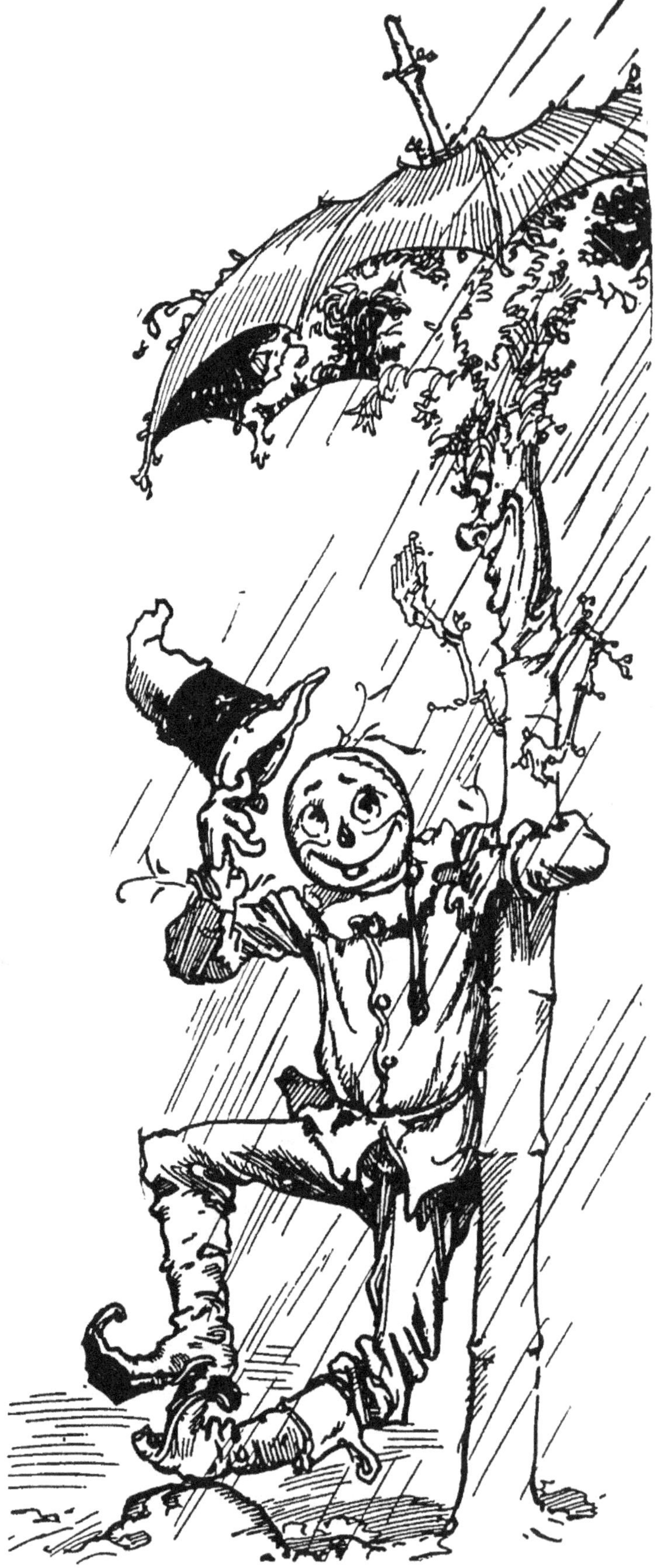

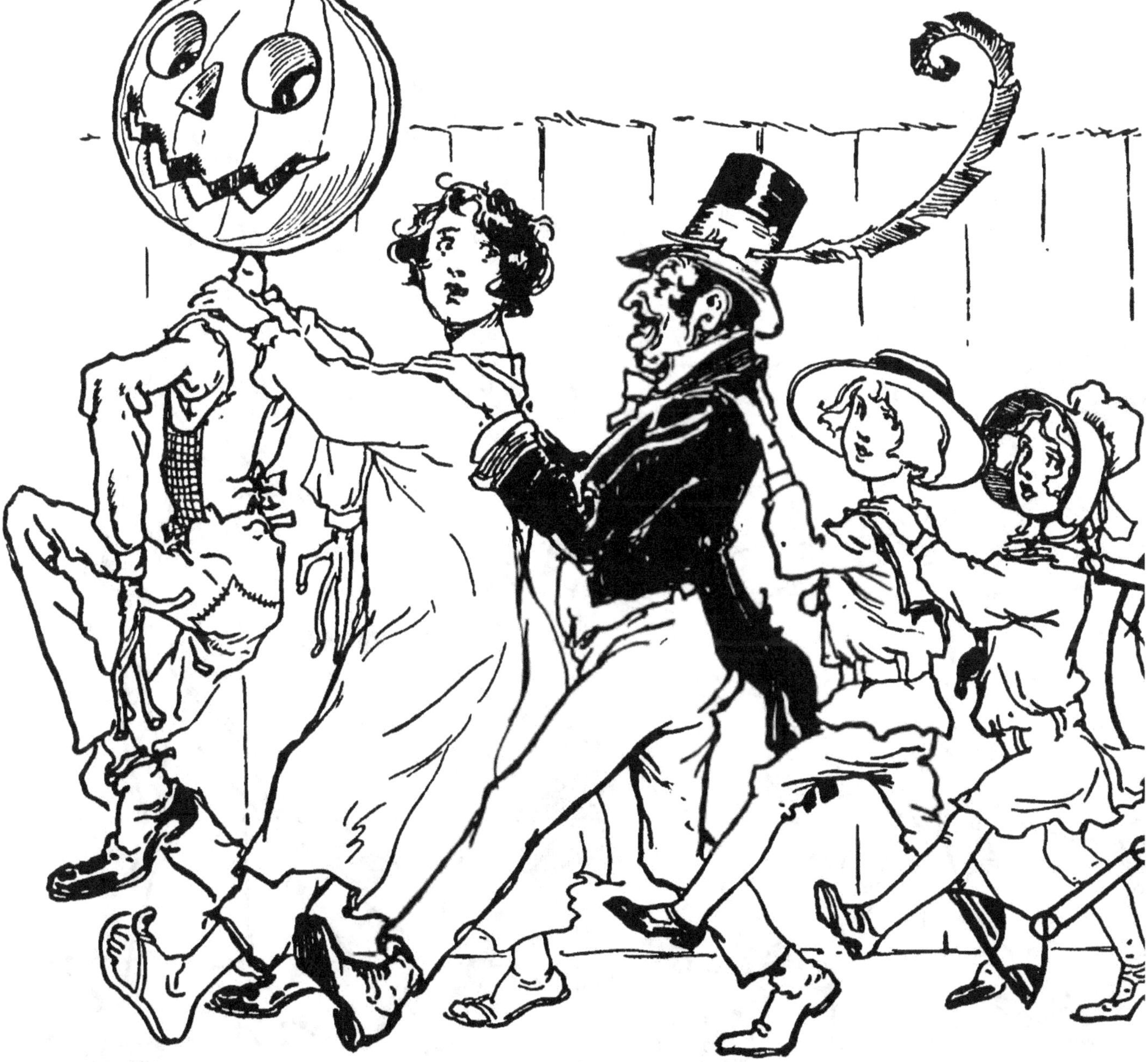

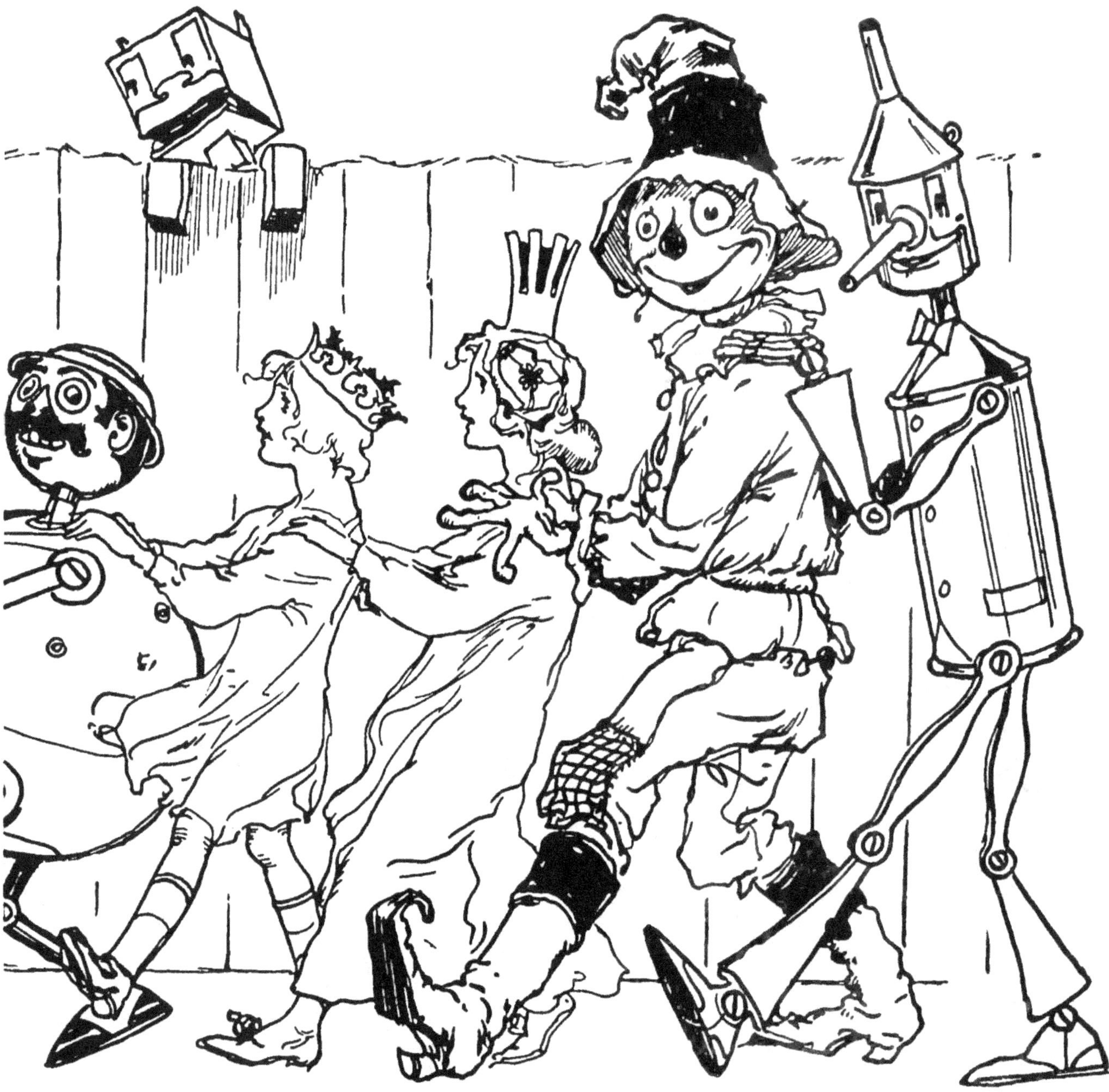

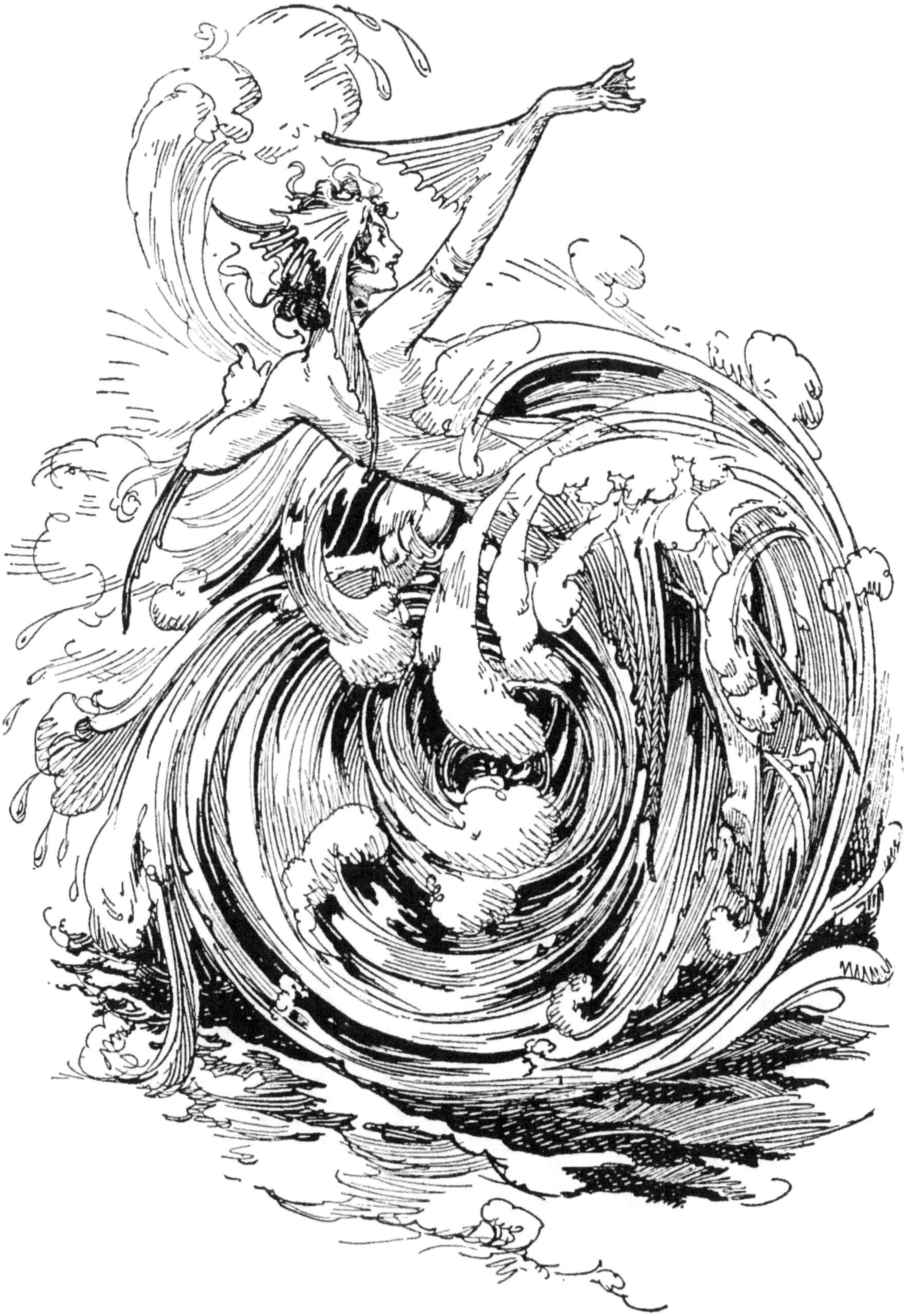

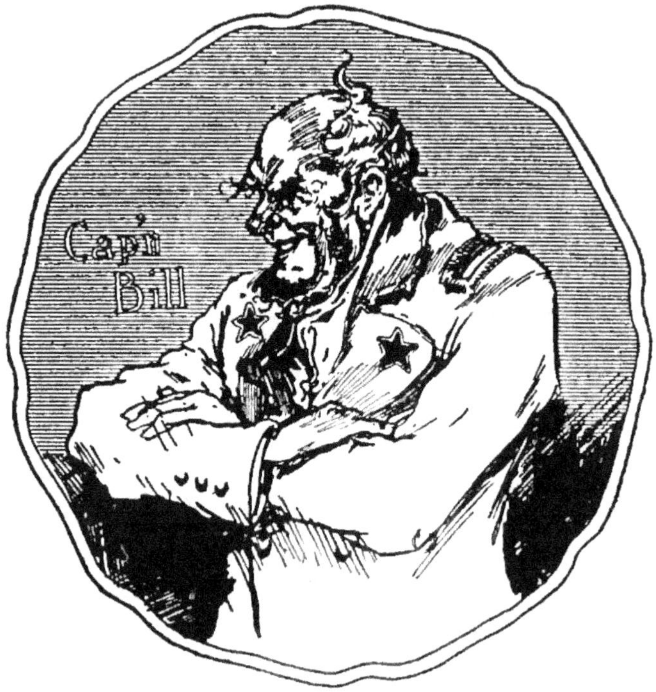
Cap'n
Bill

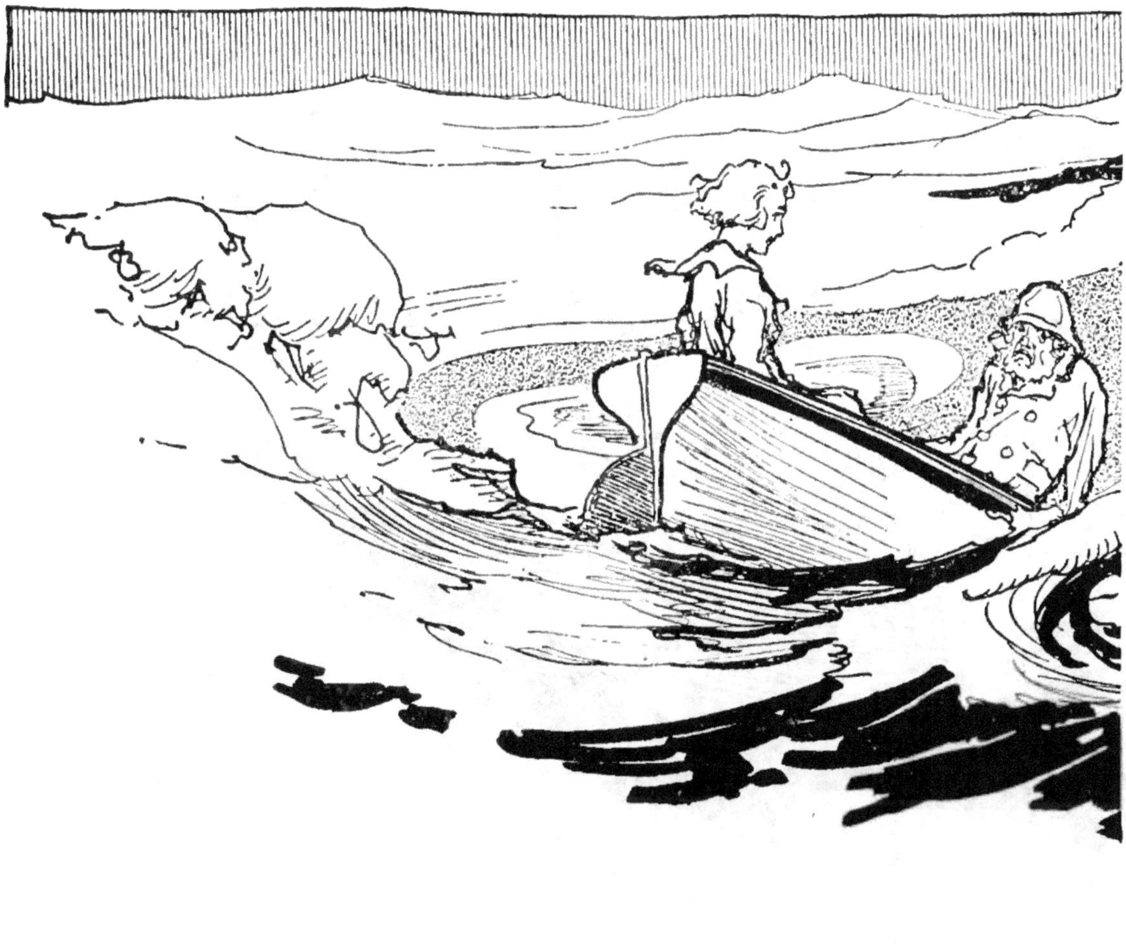

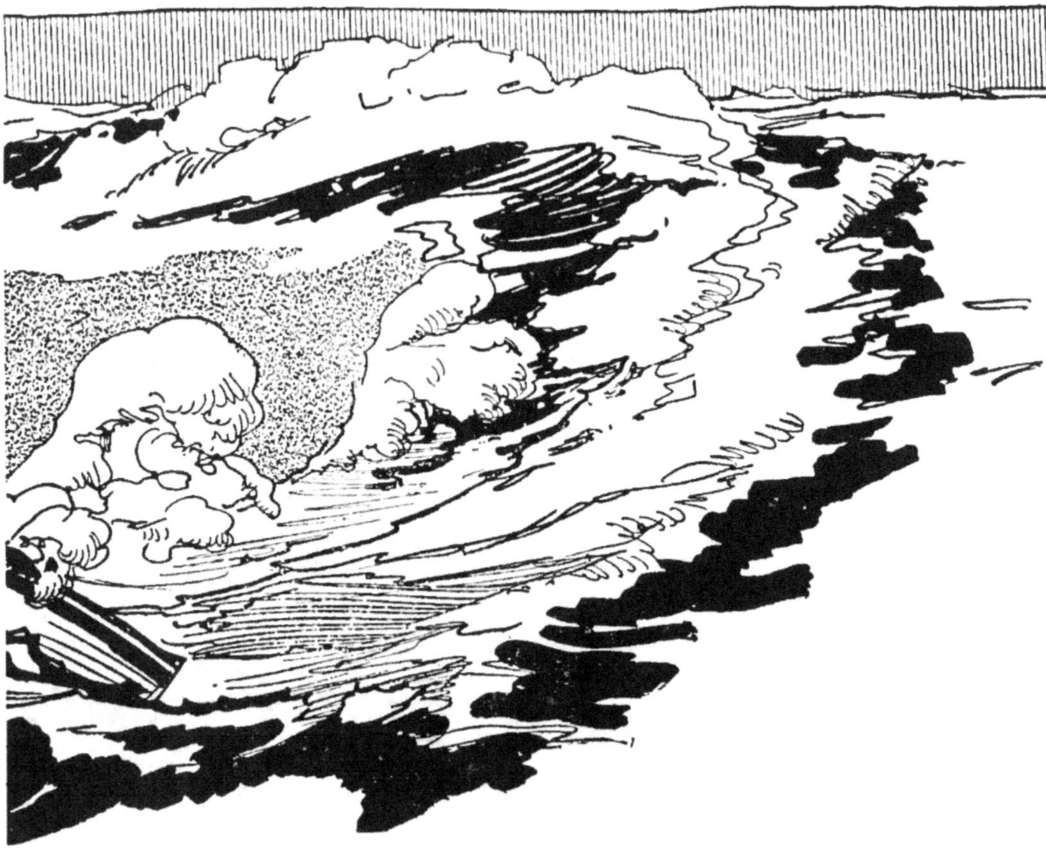

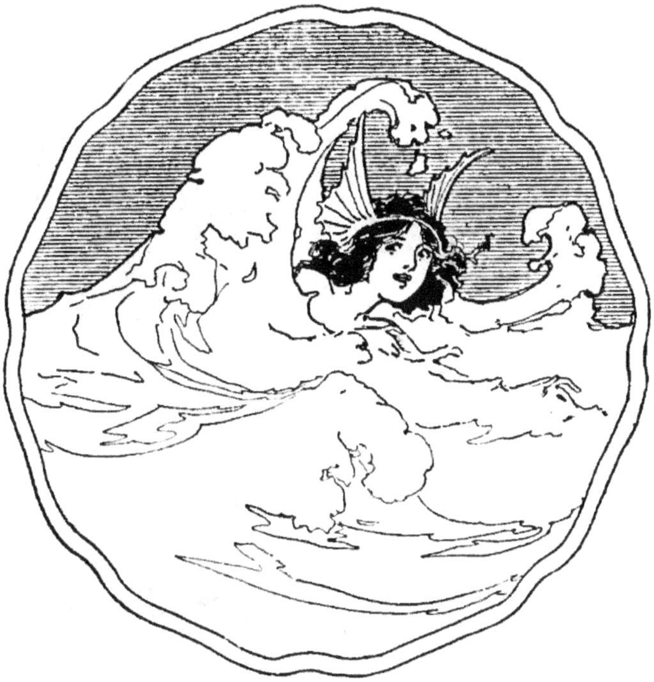

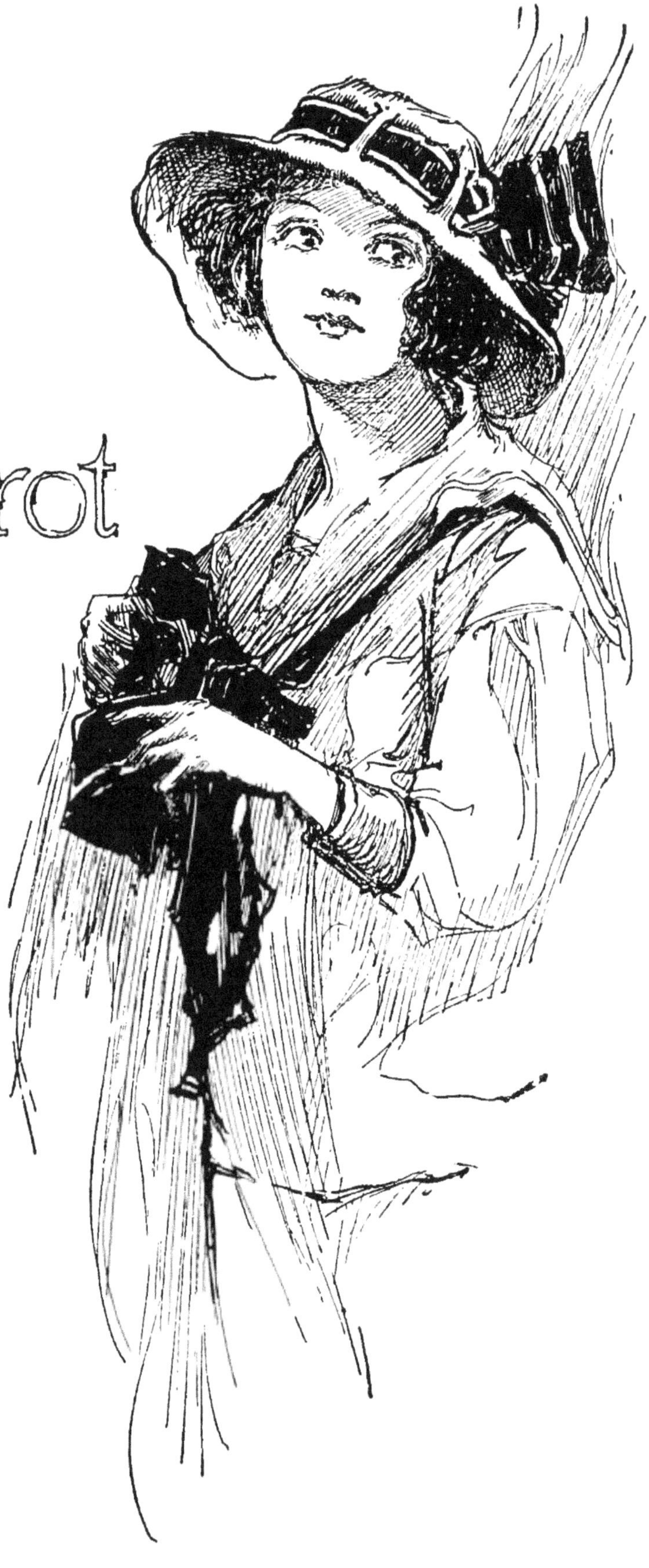

Trot

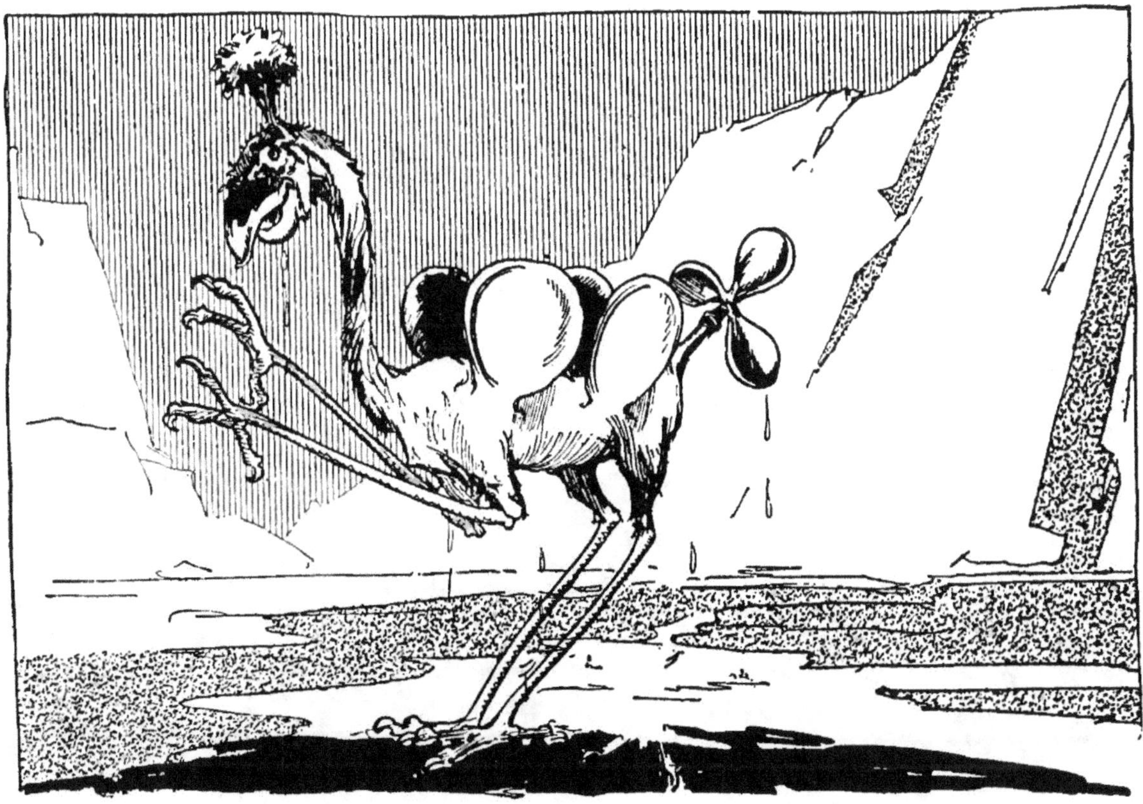

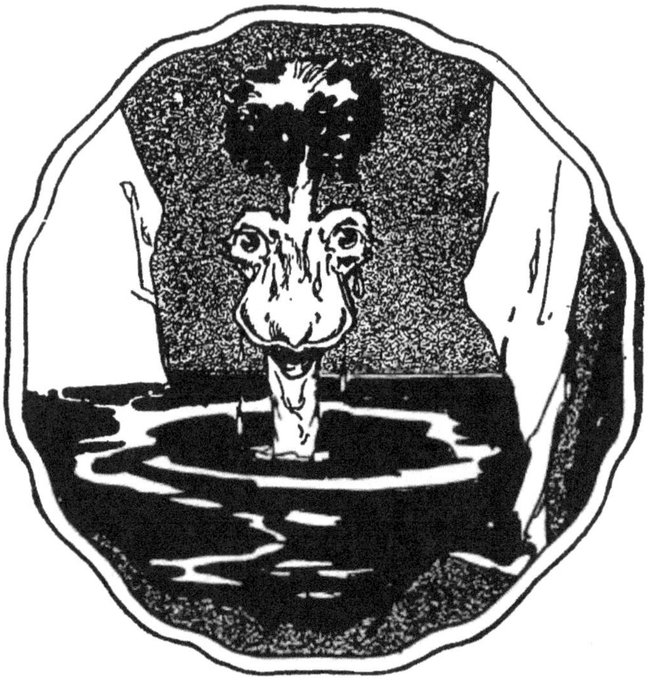

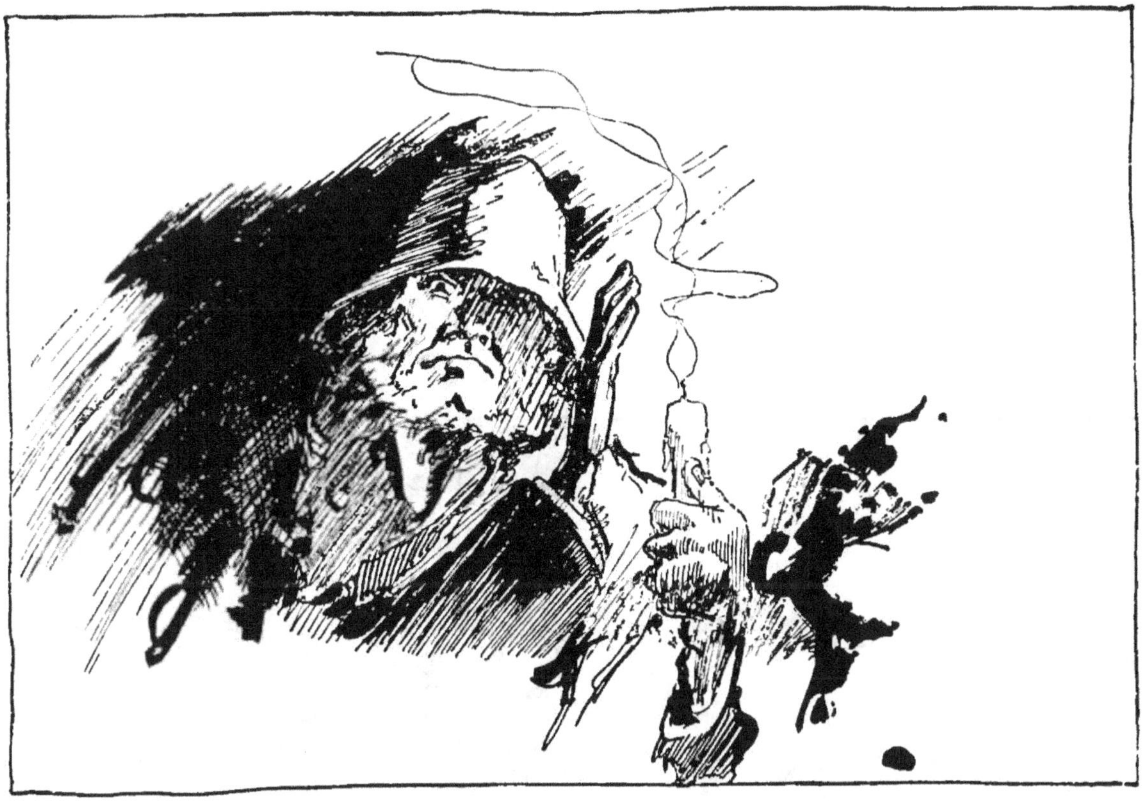

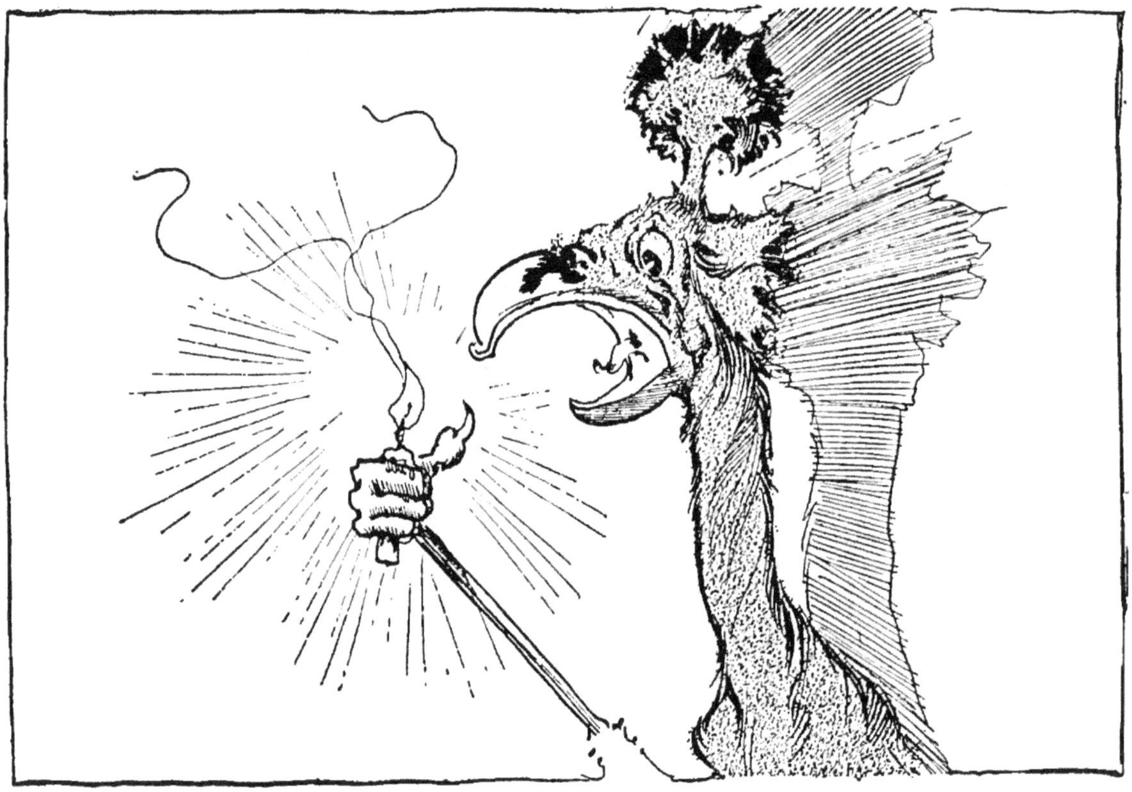

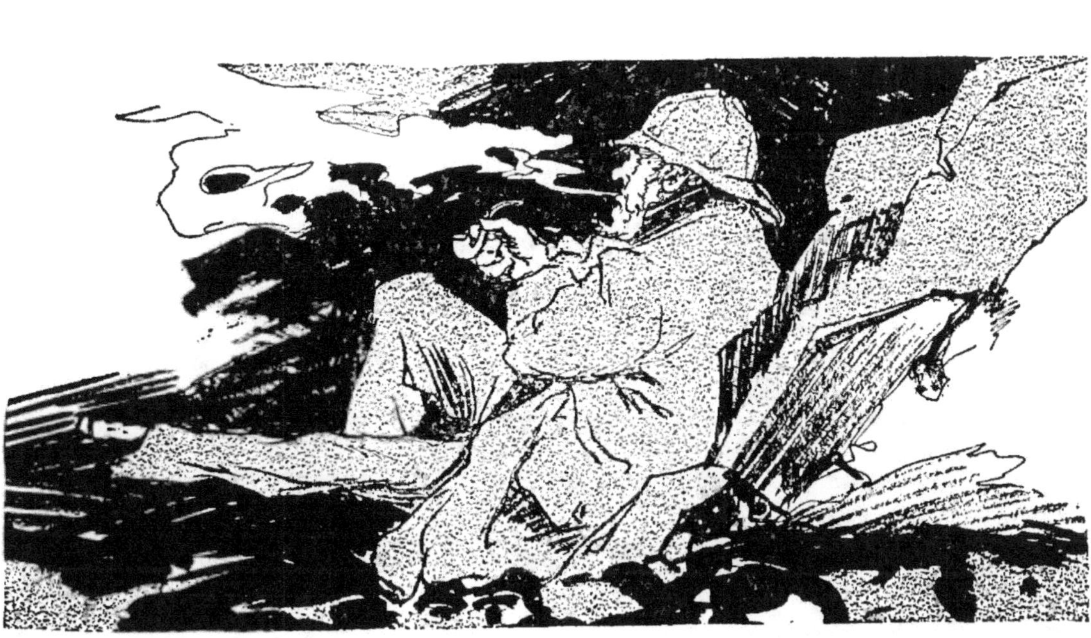

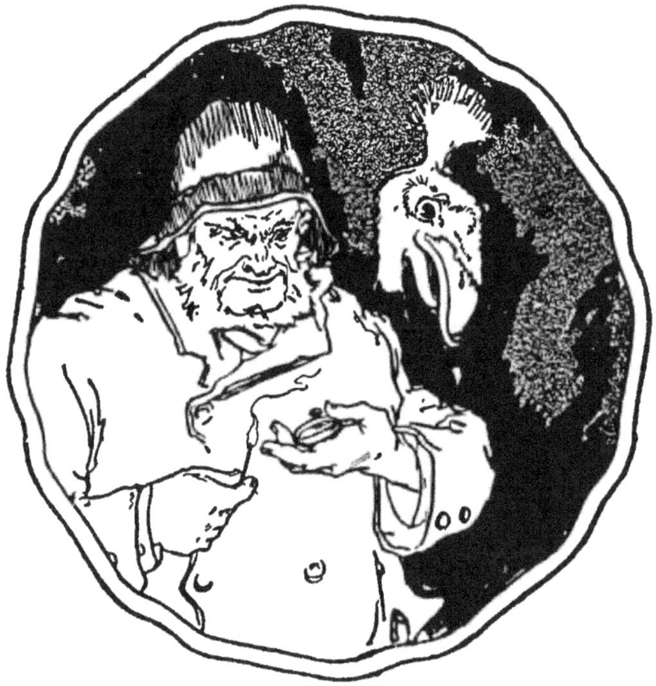

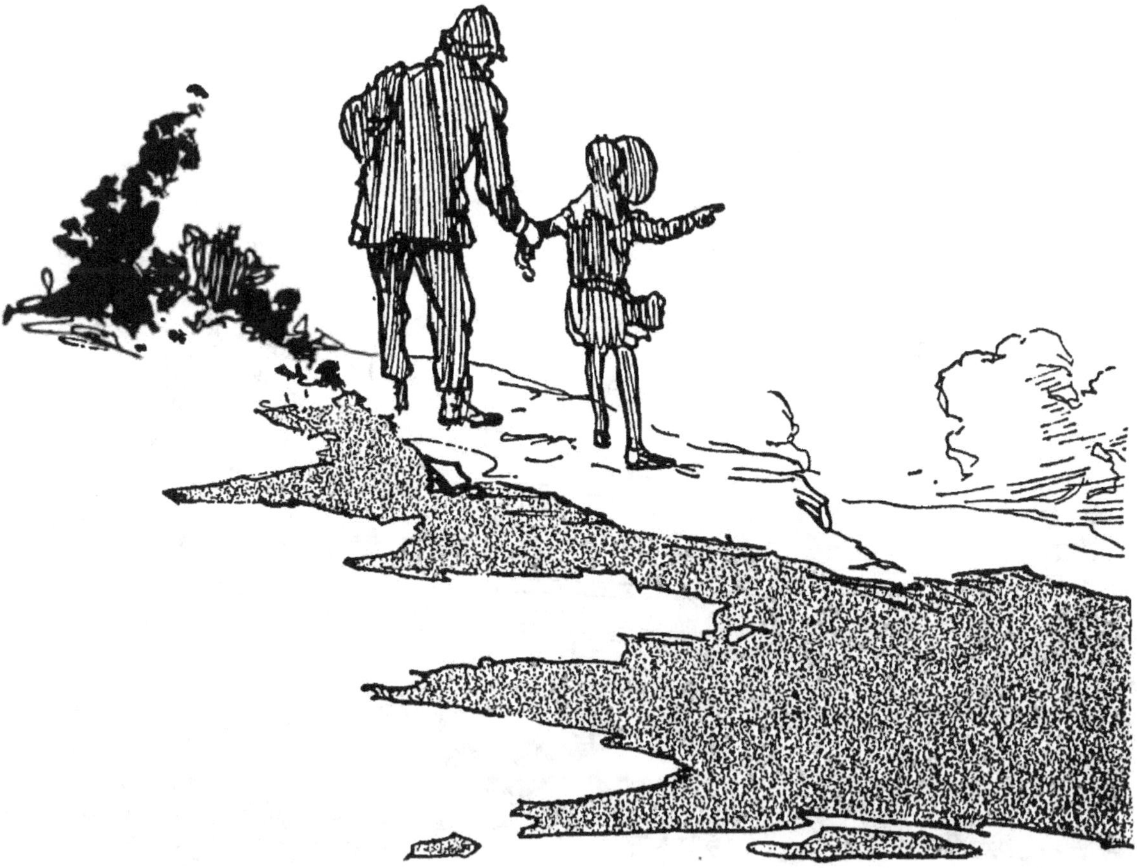

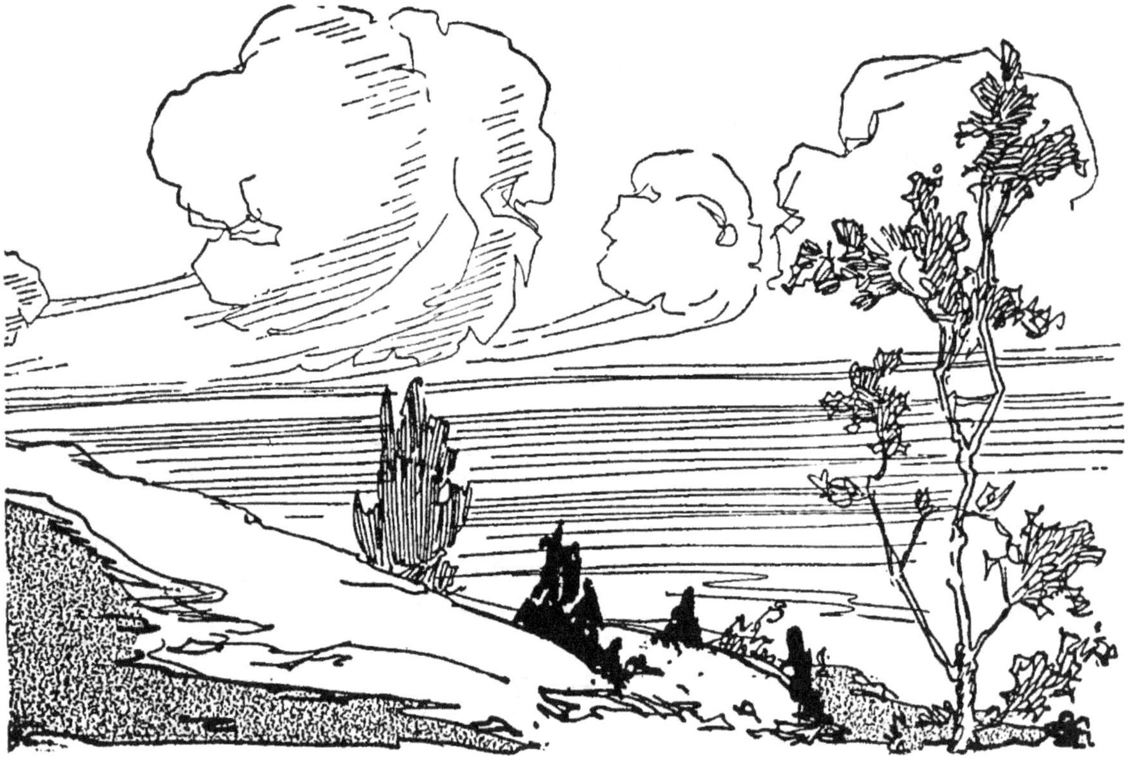

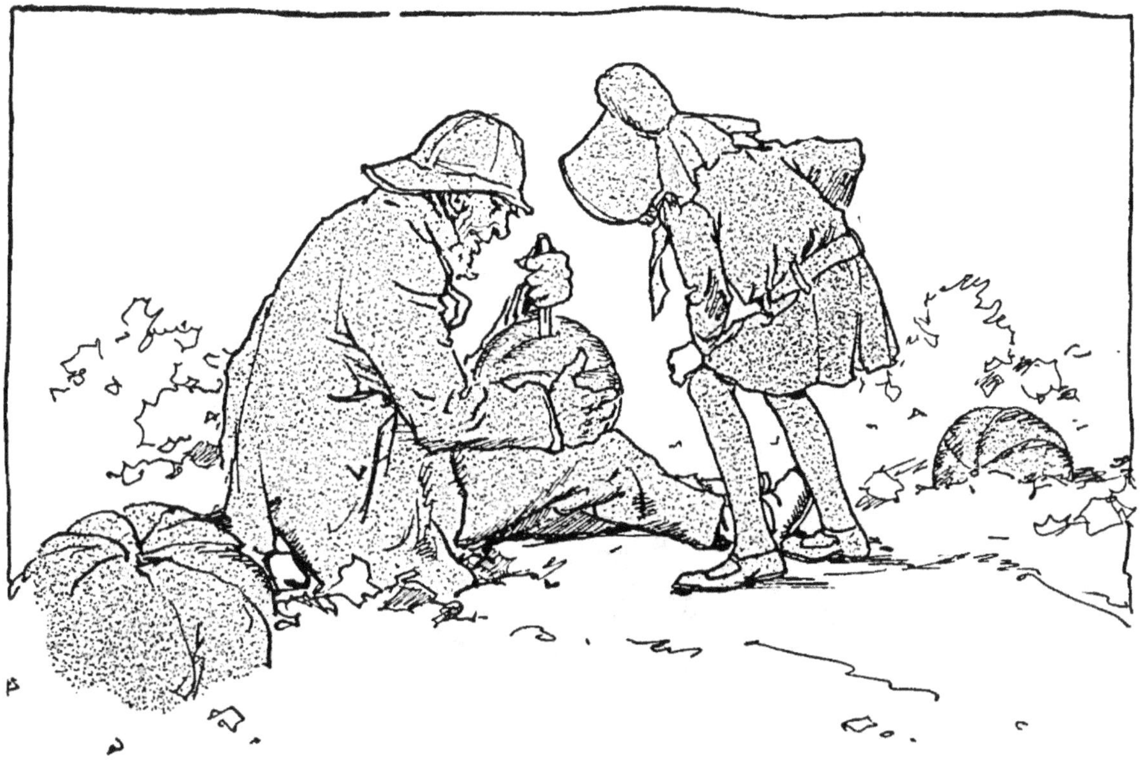

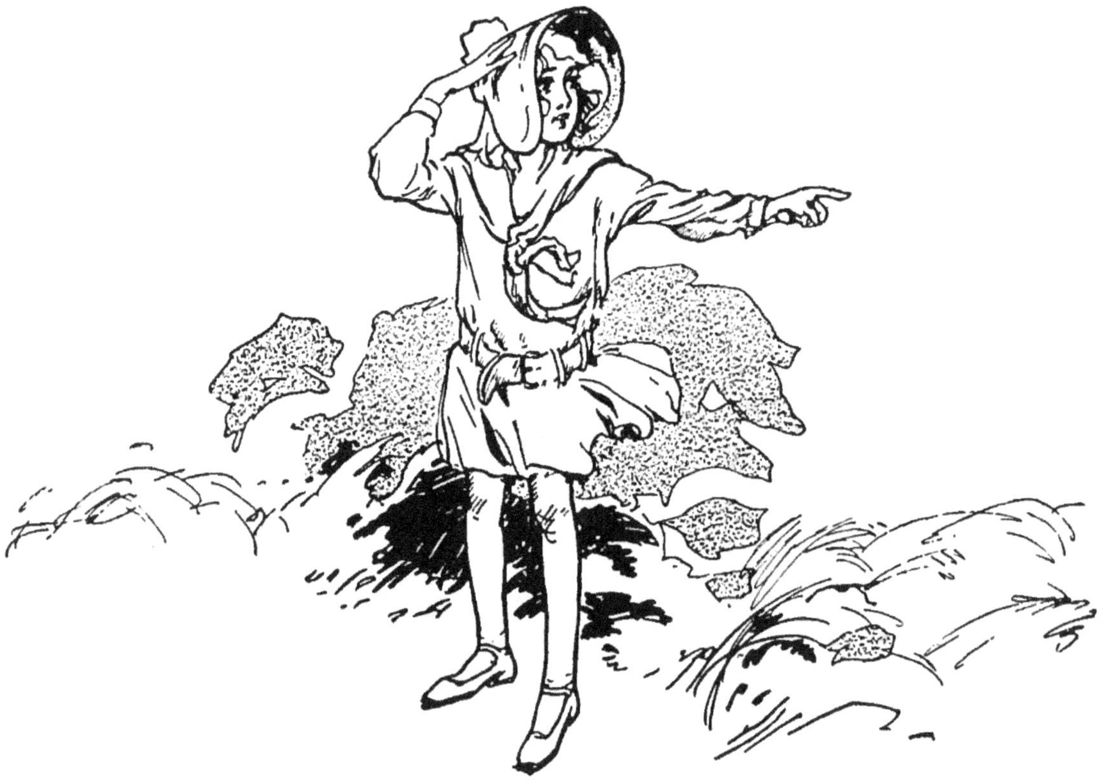

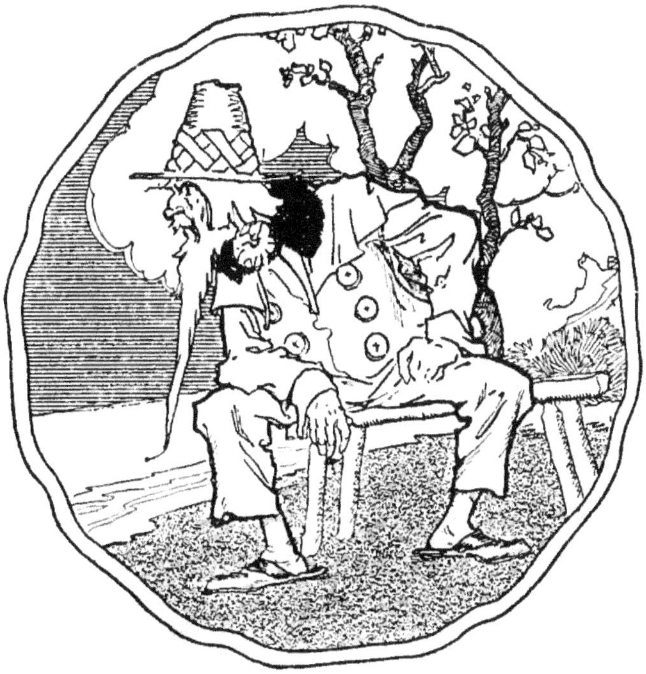

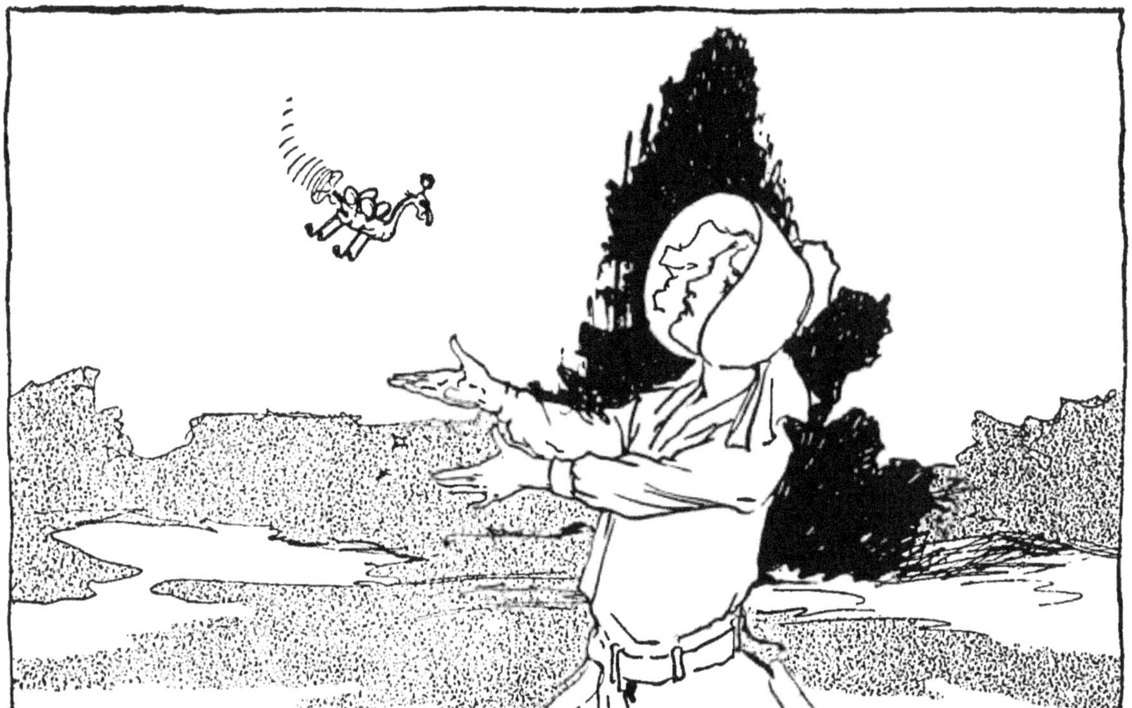

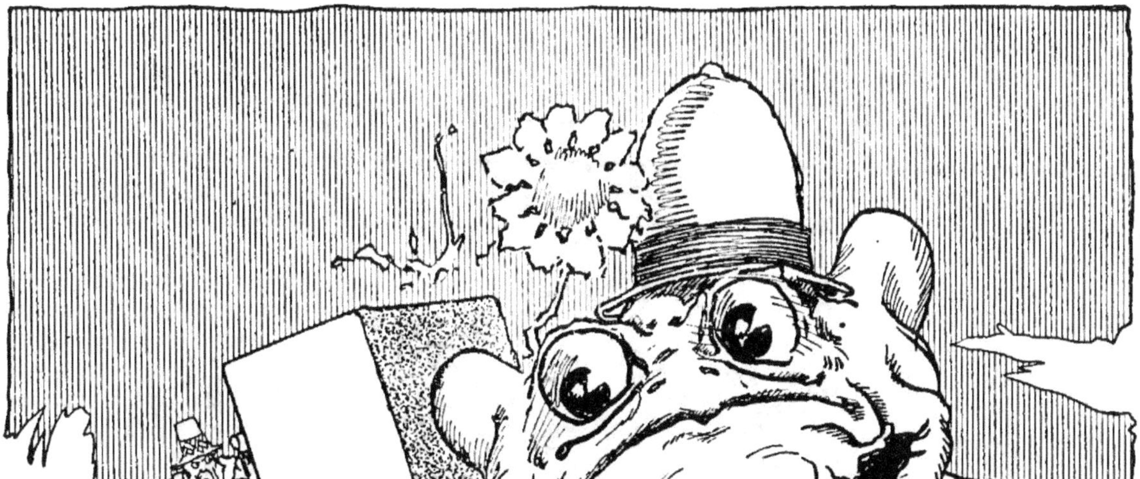

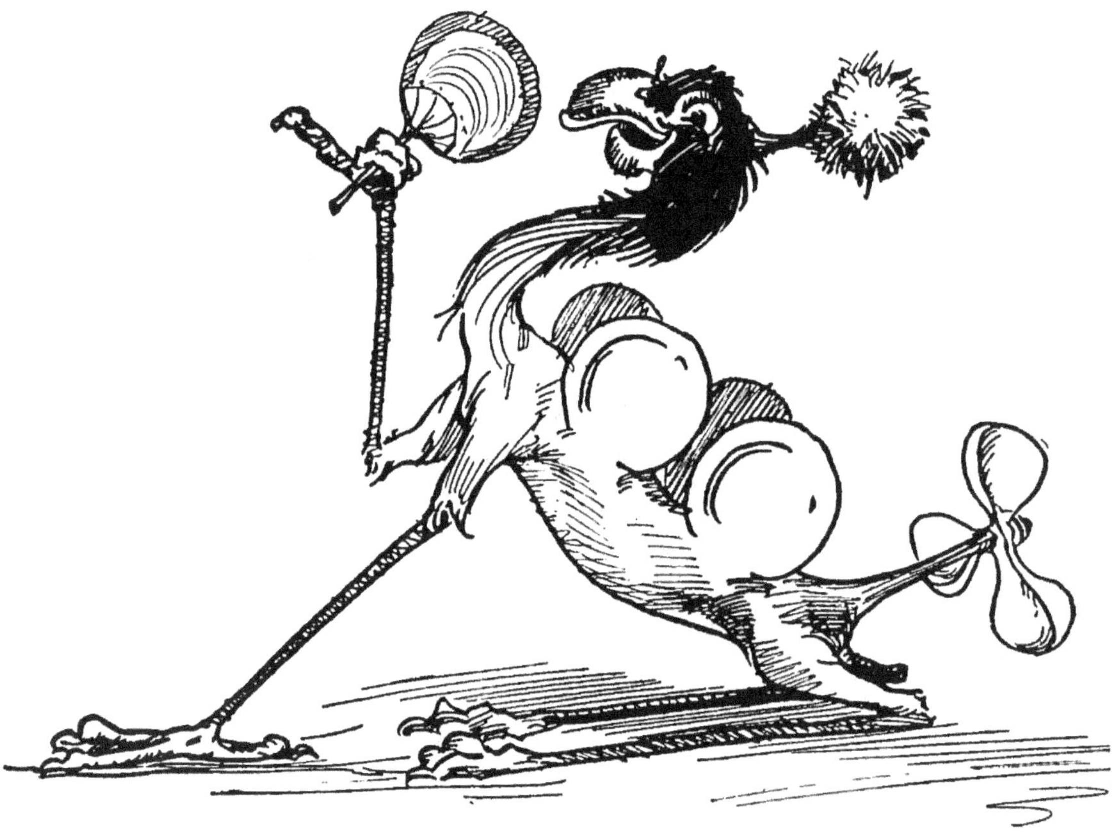

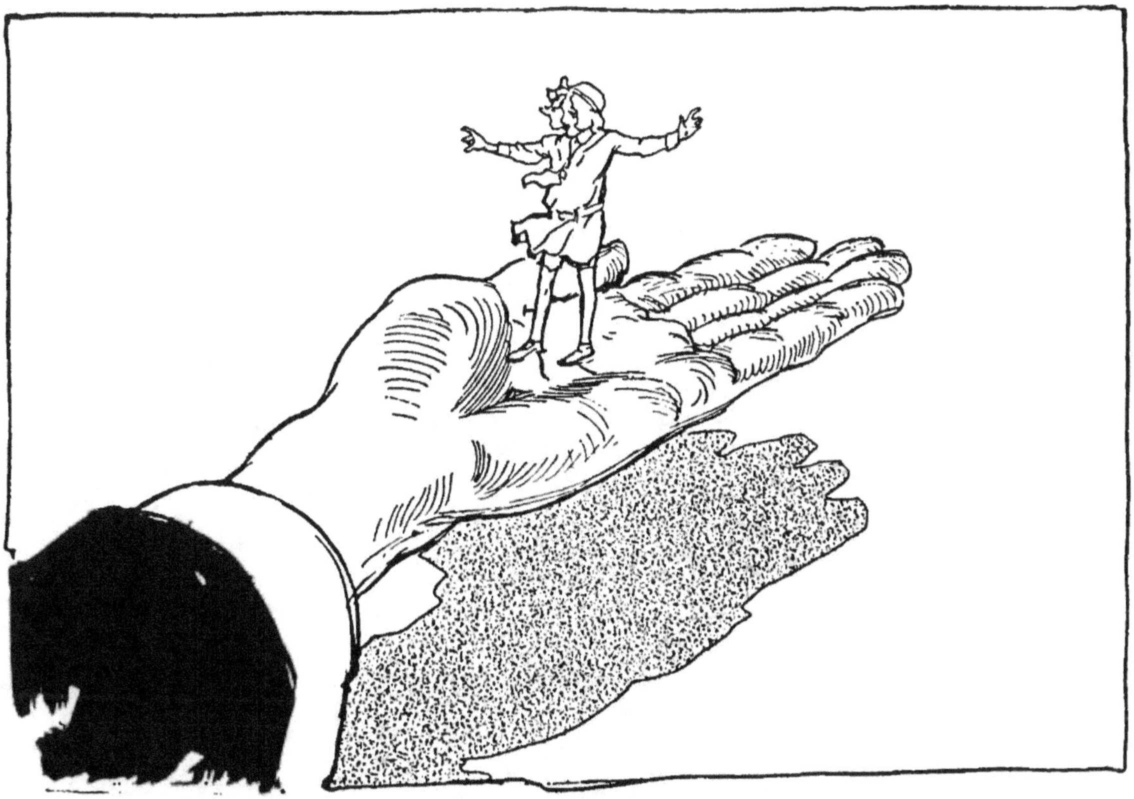

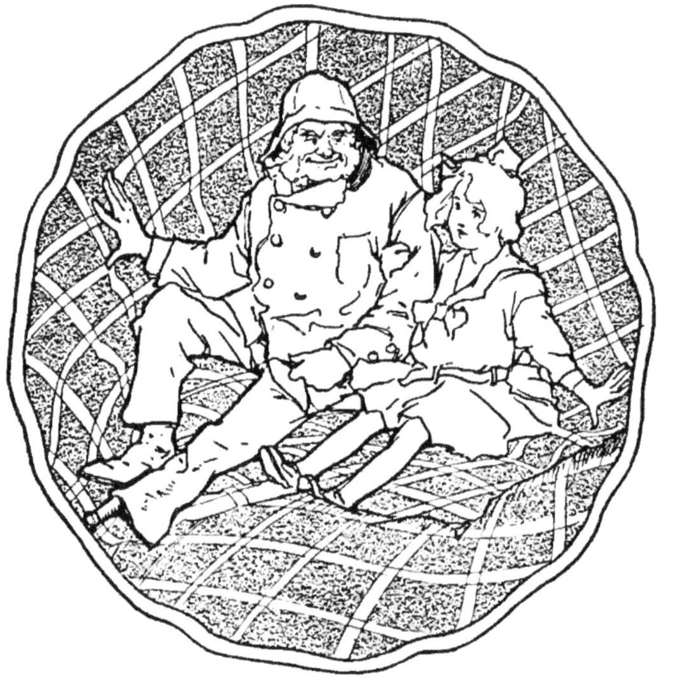

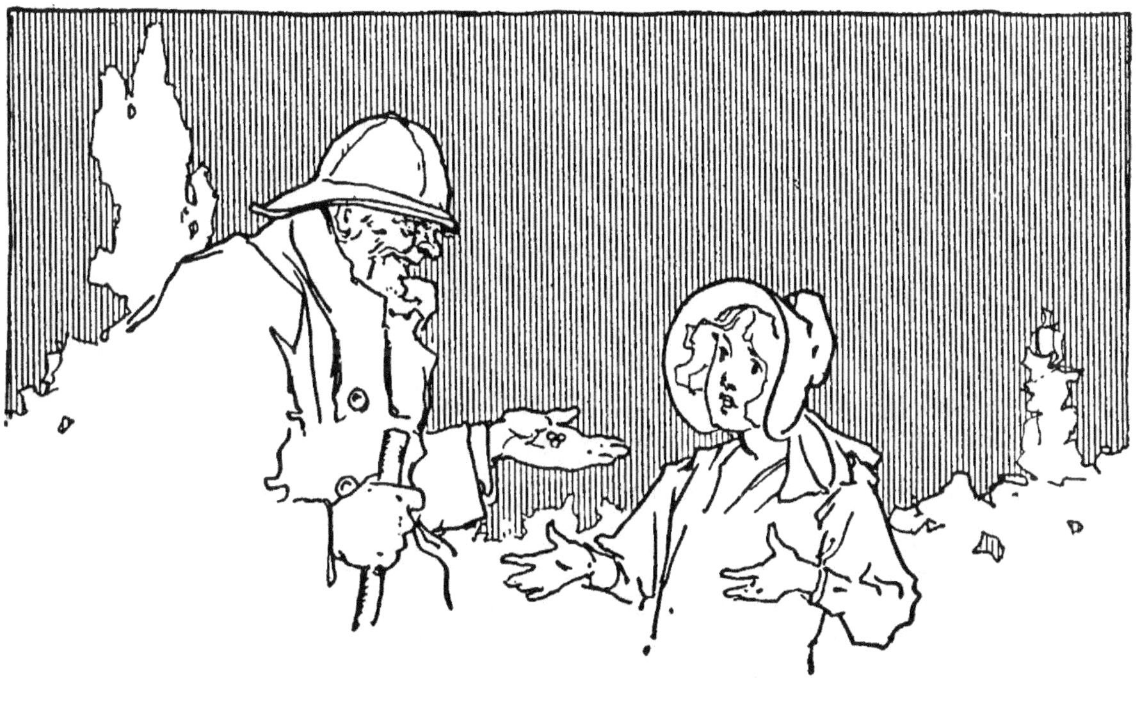

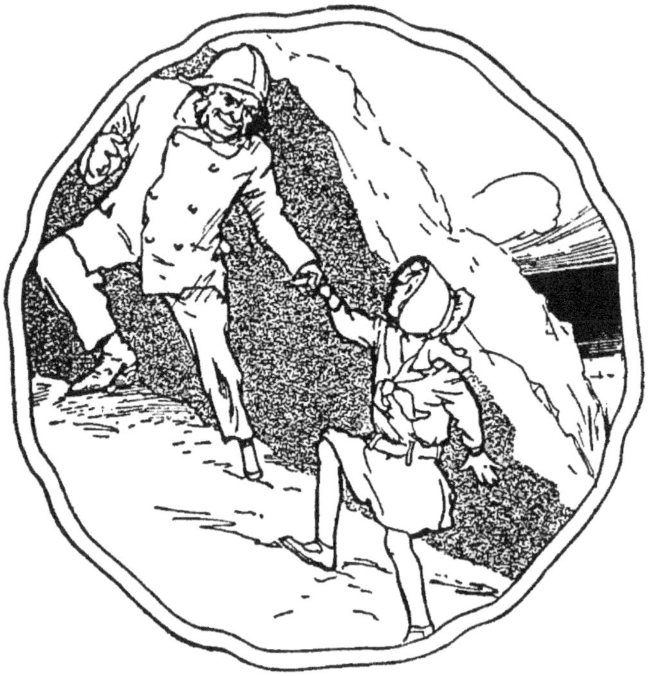

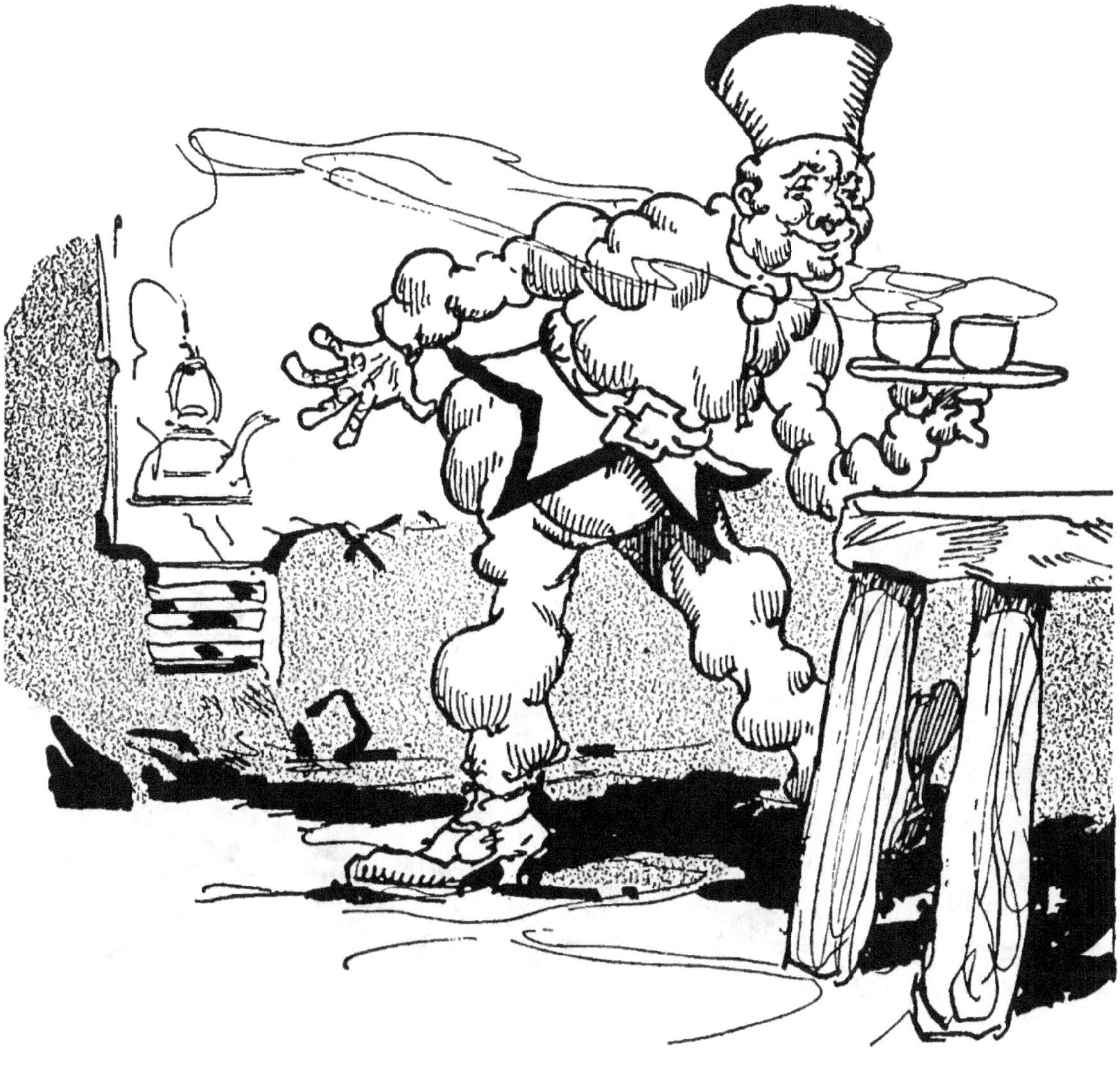

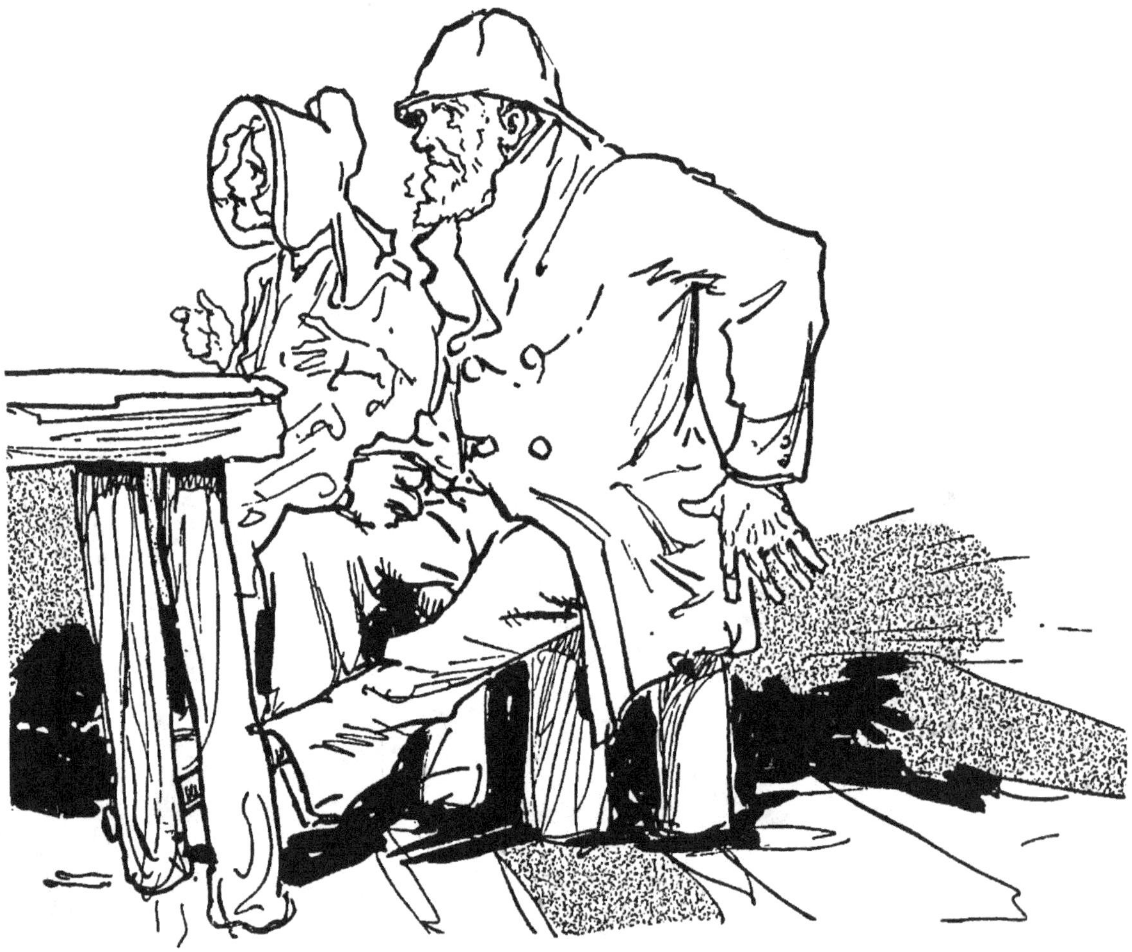

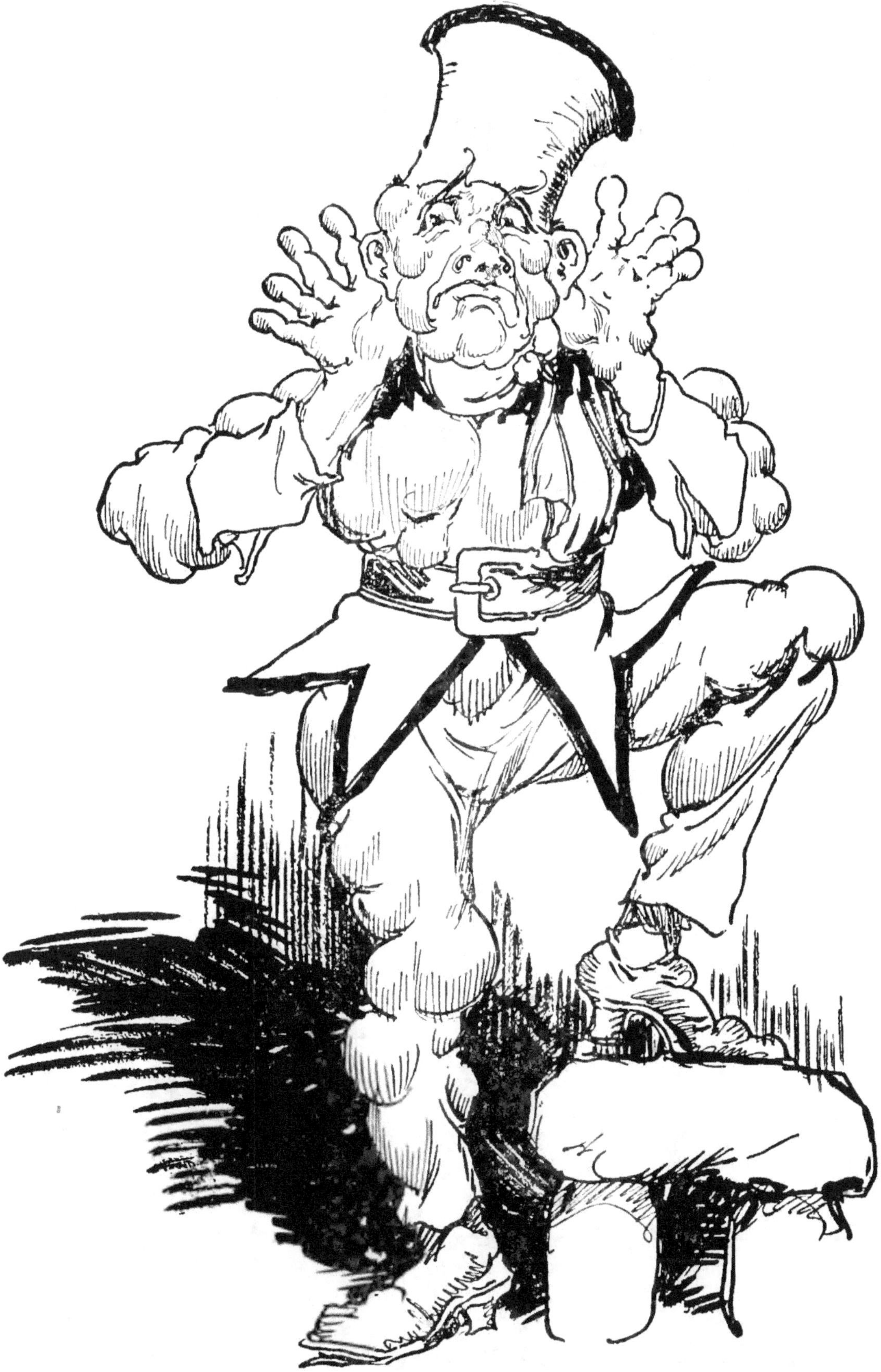

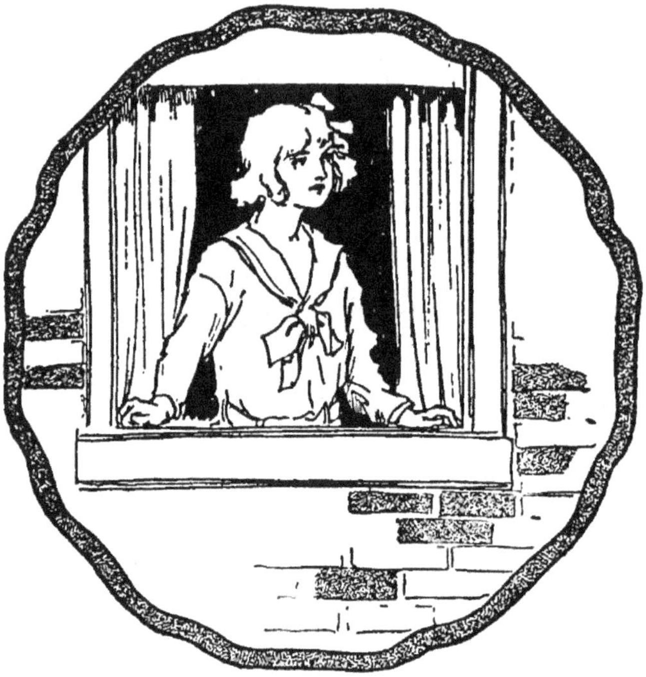

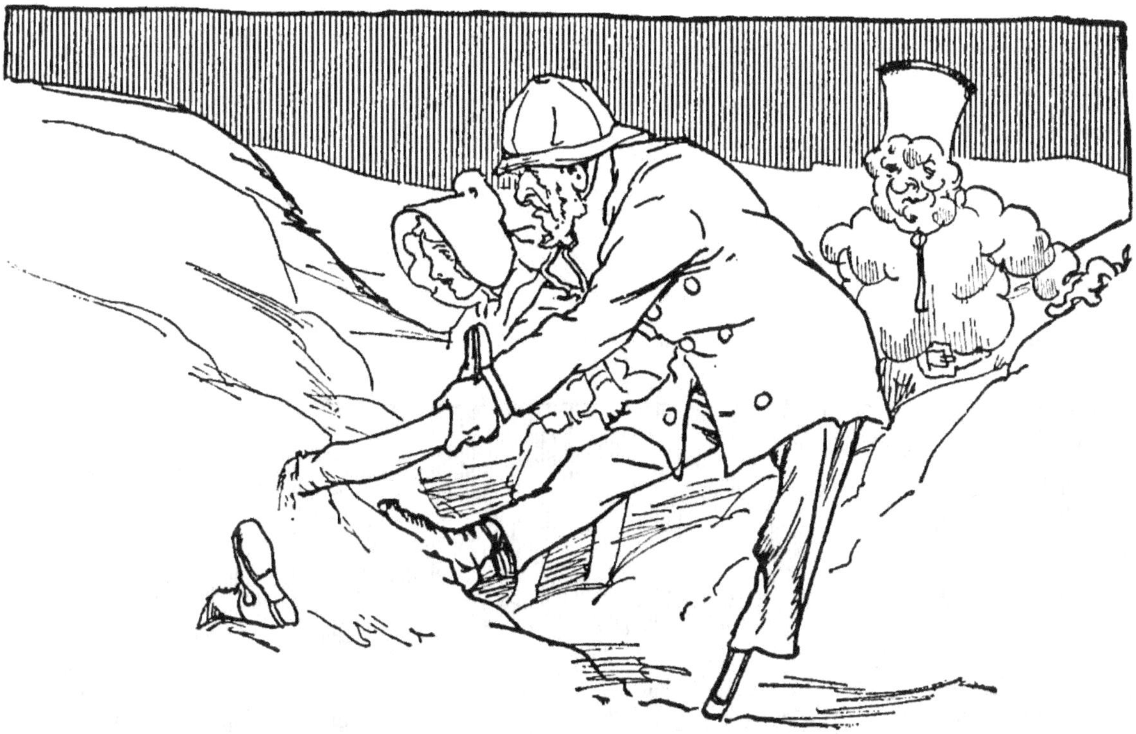

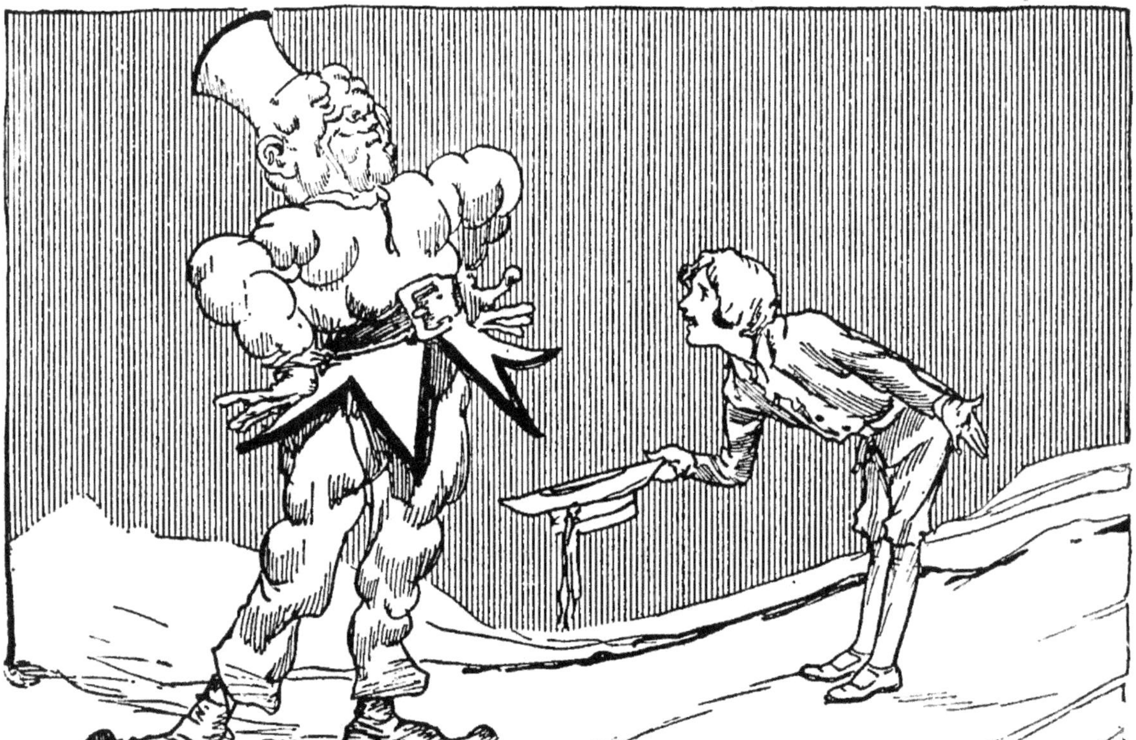

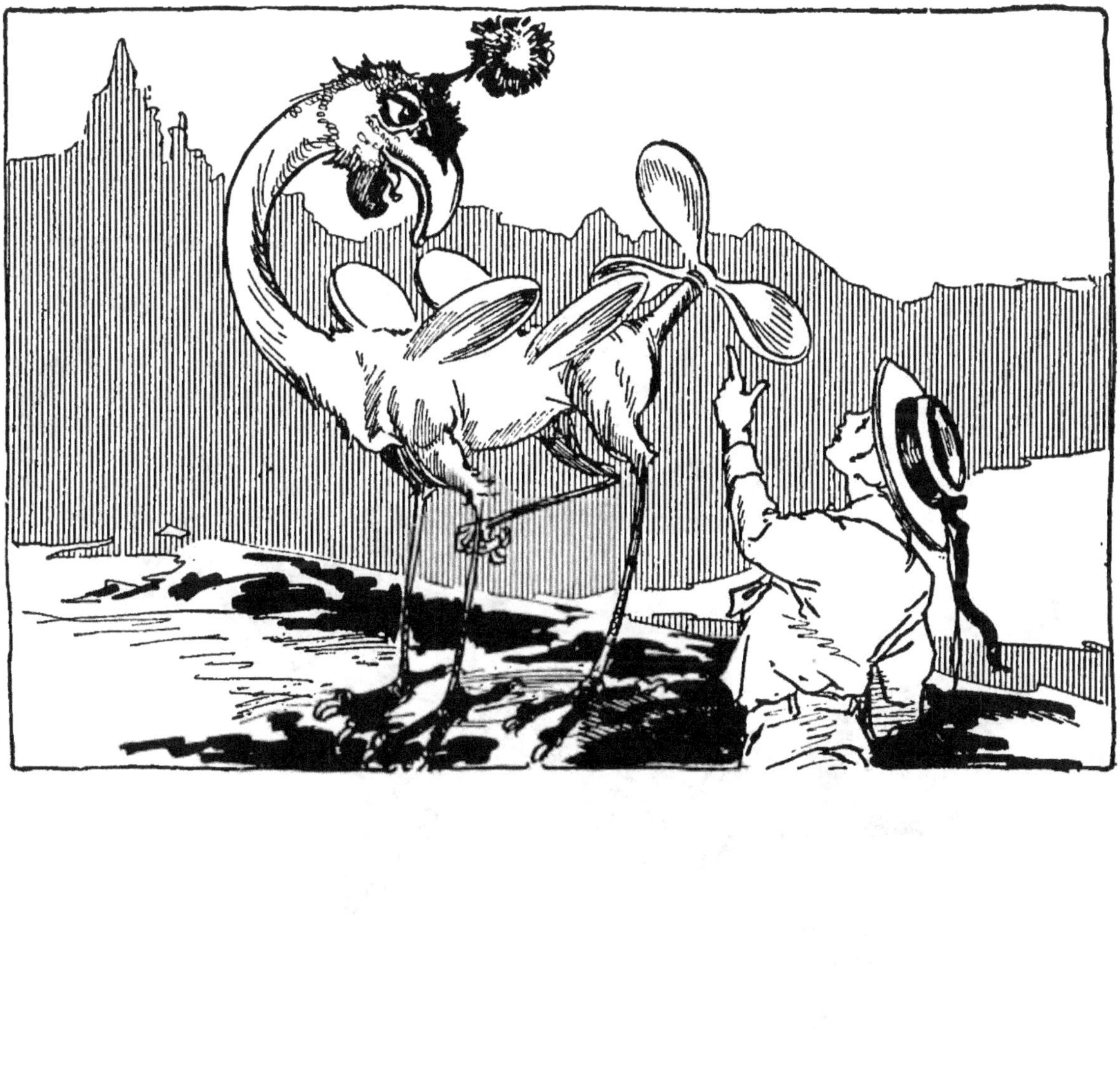

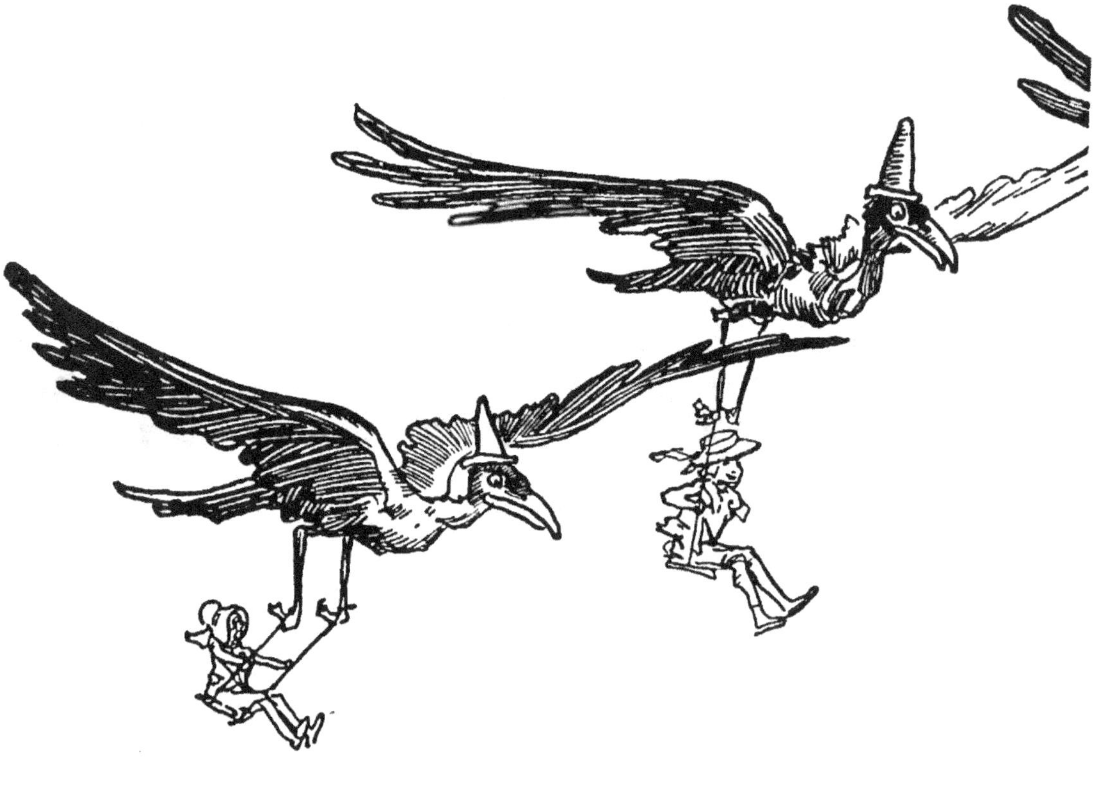

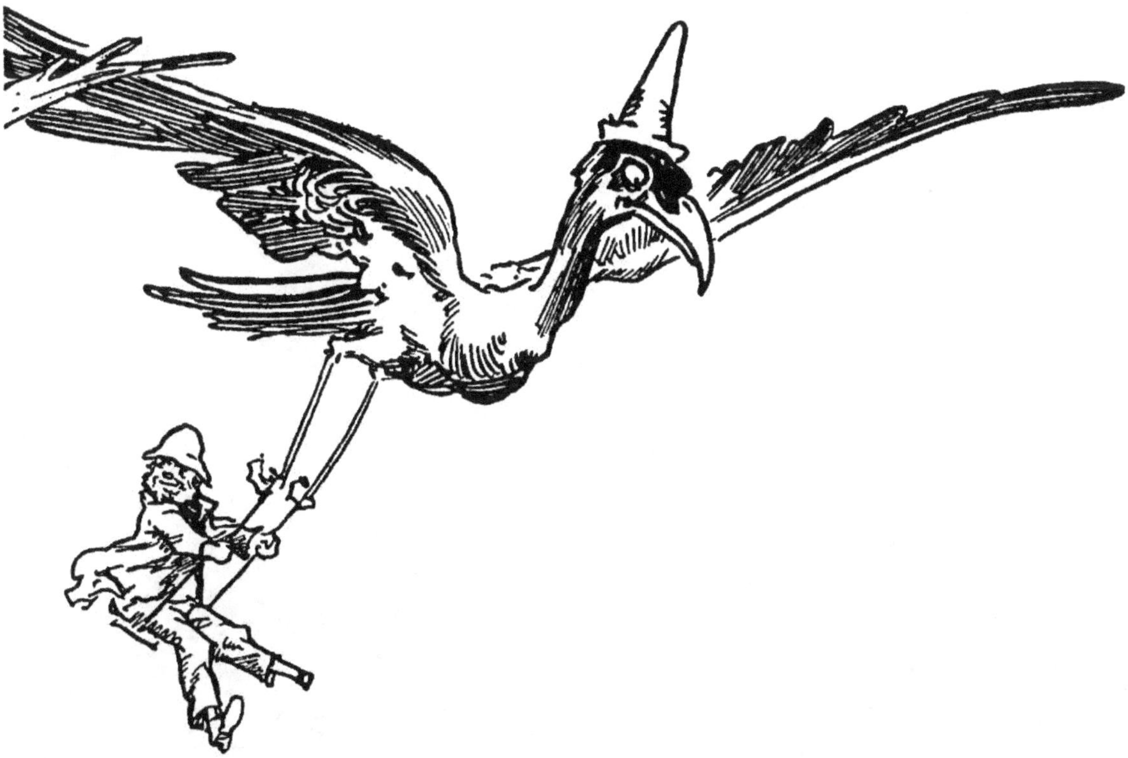

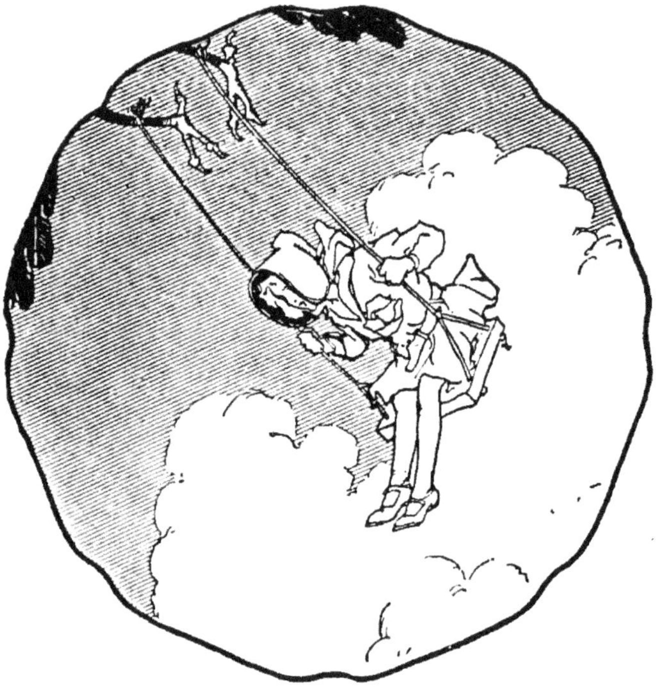

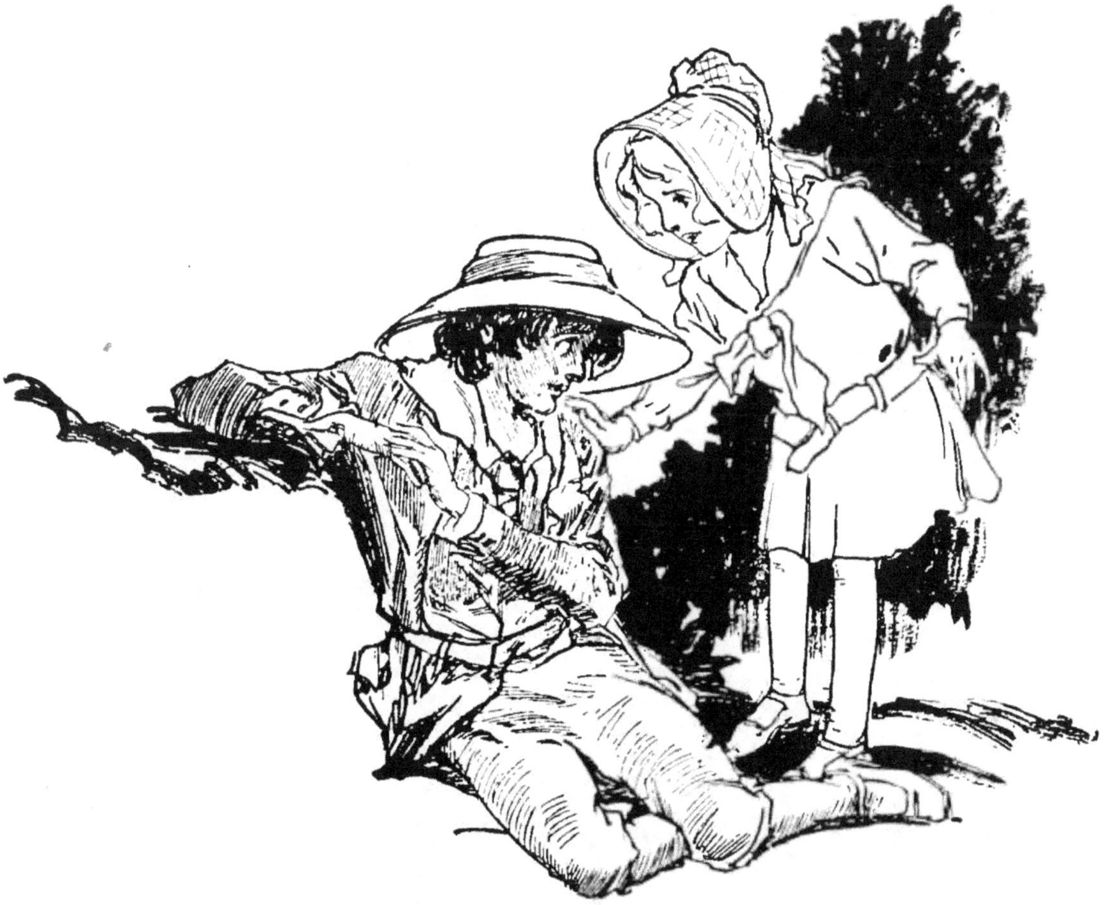

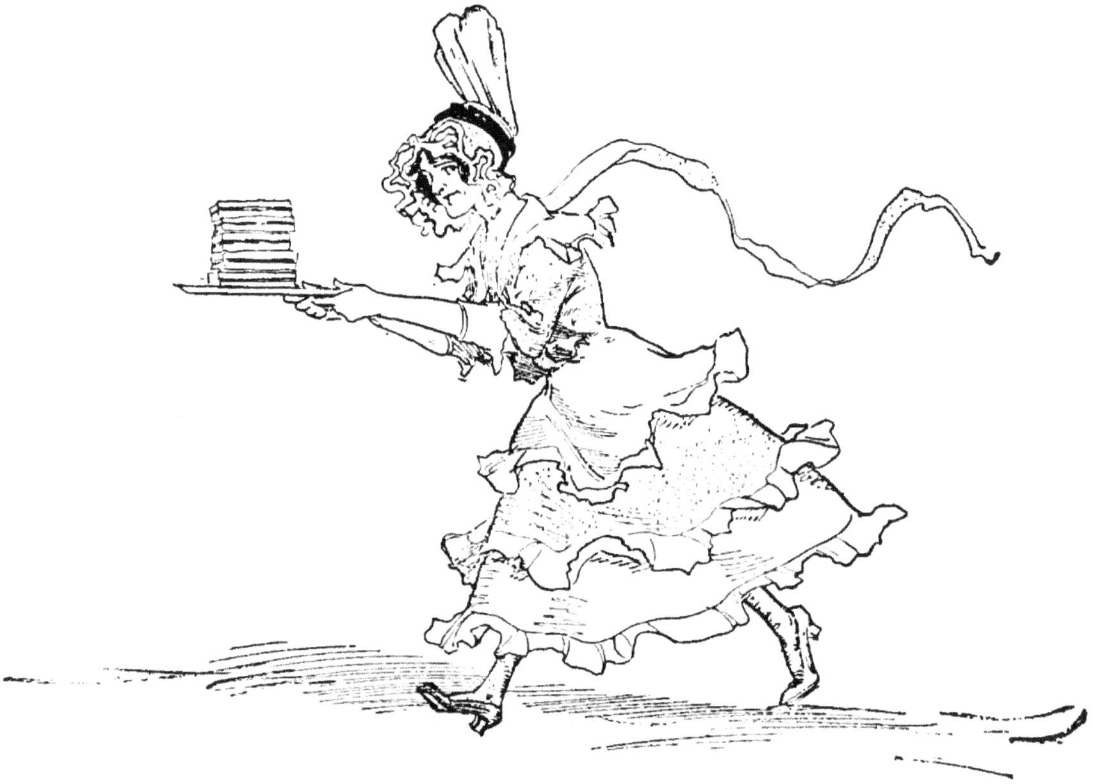

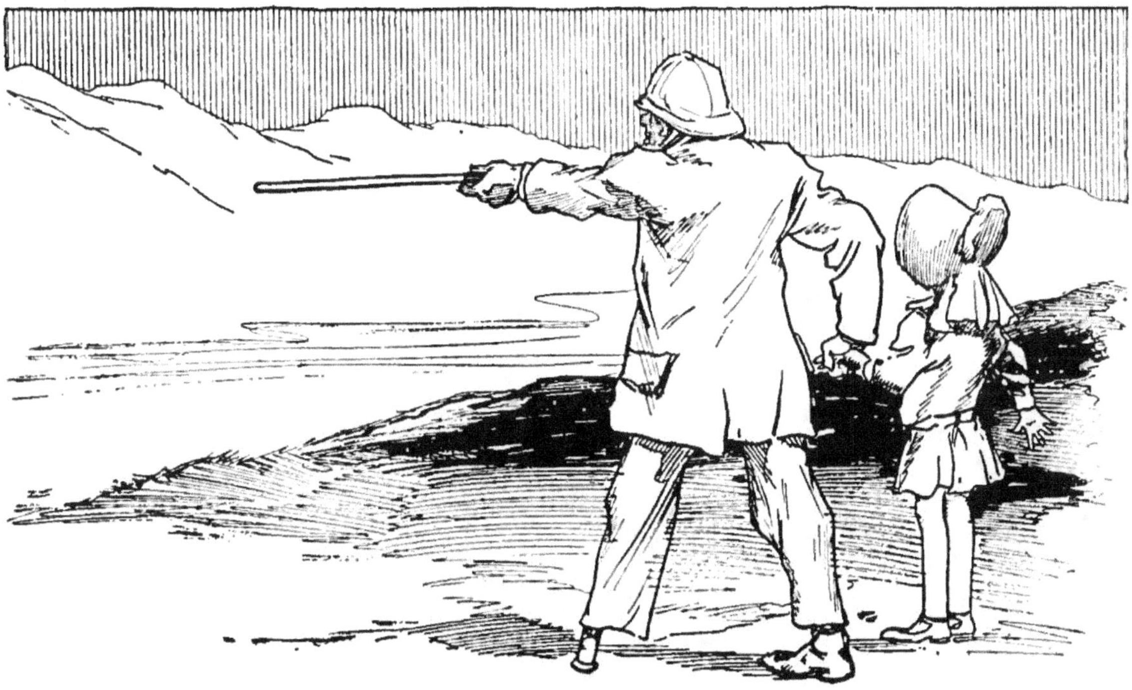

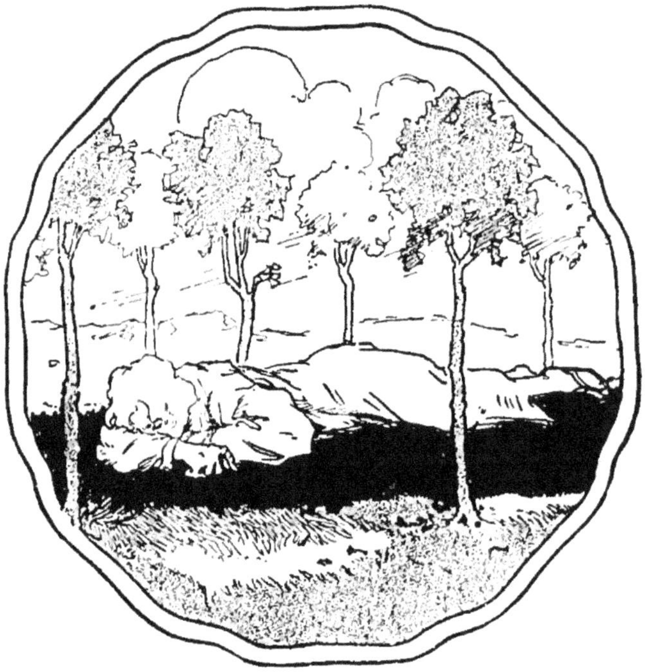

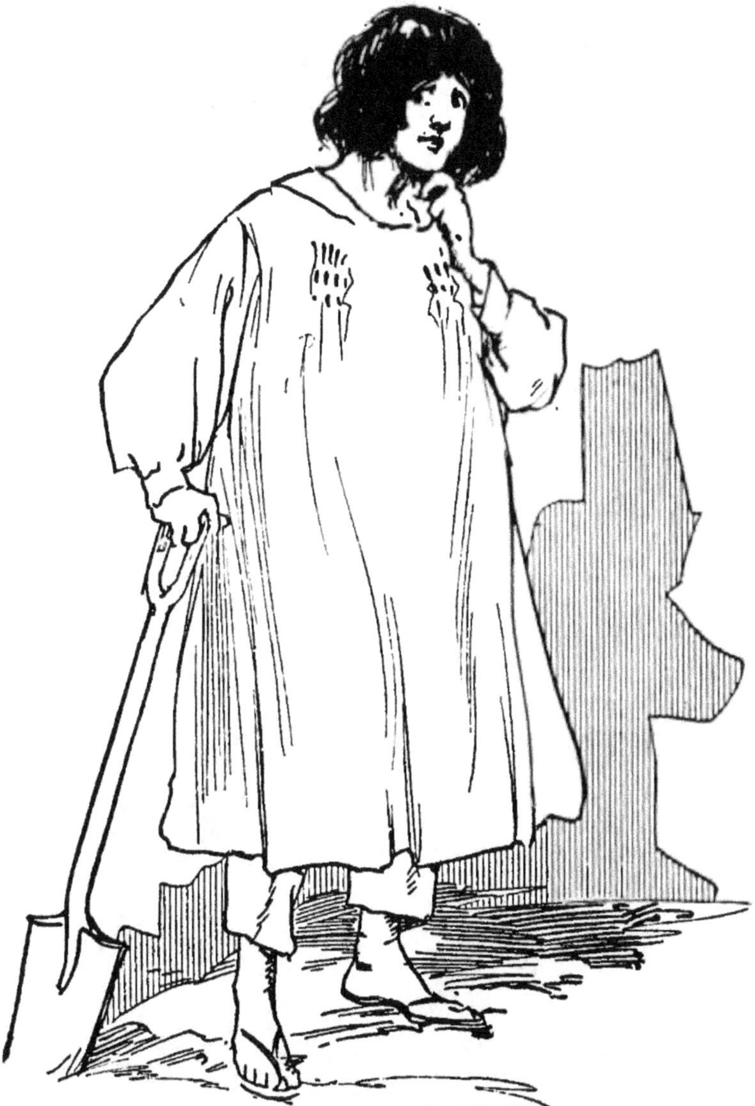

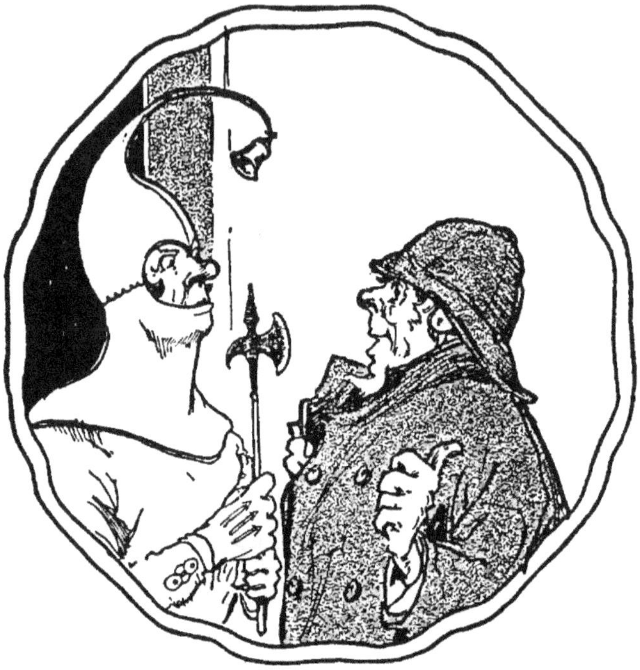

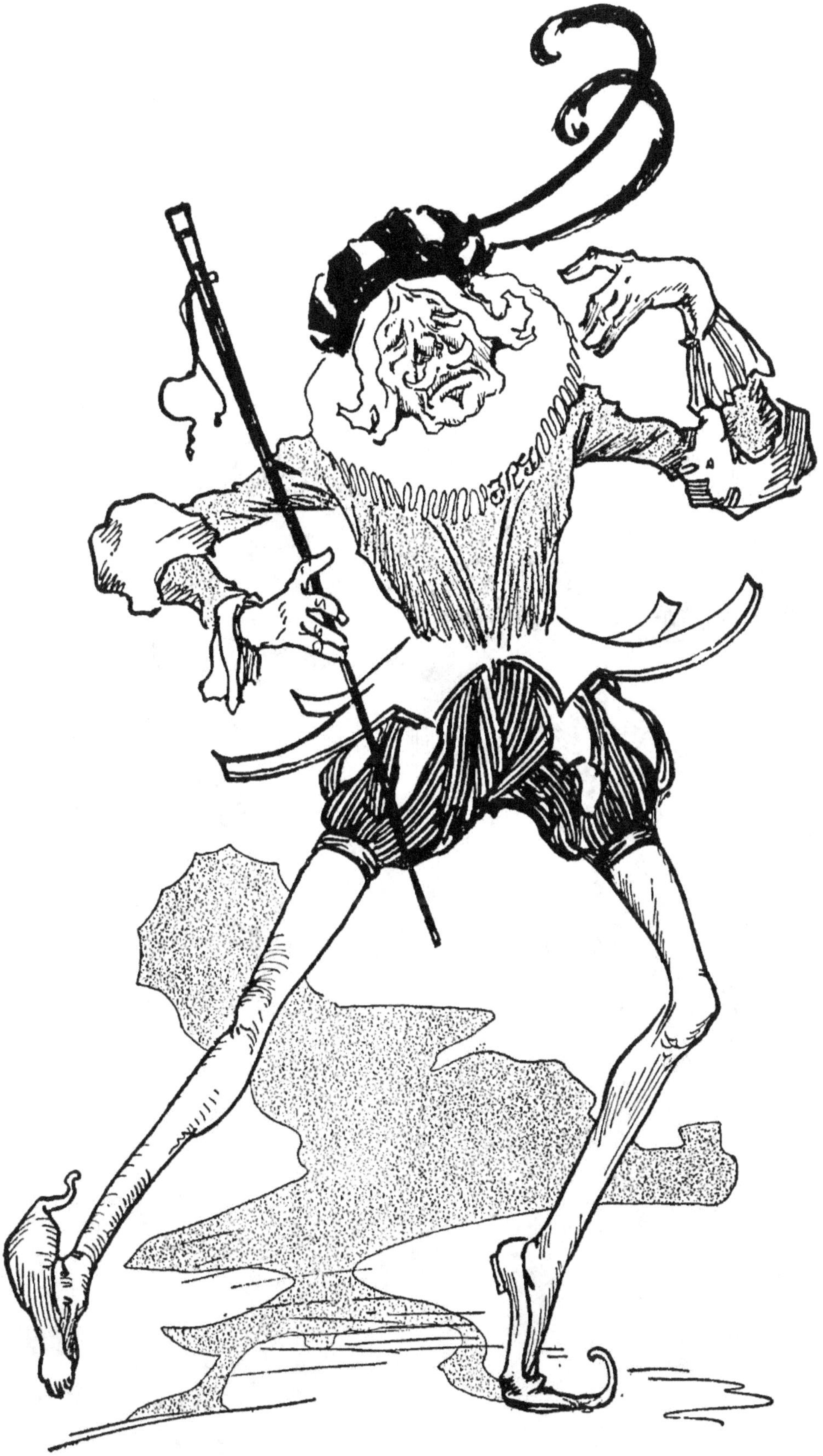

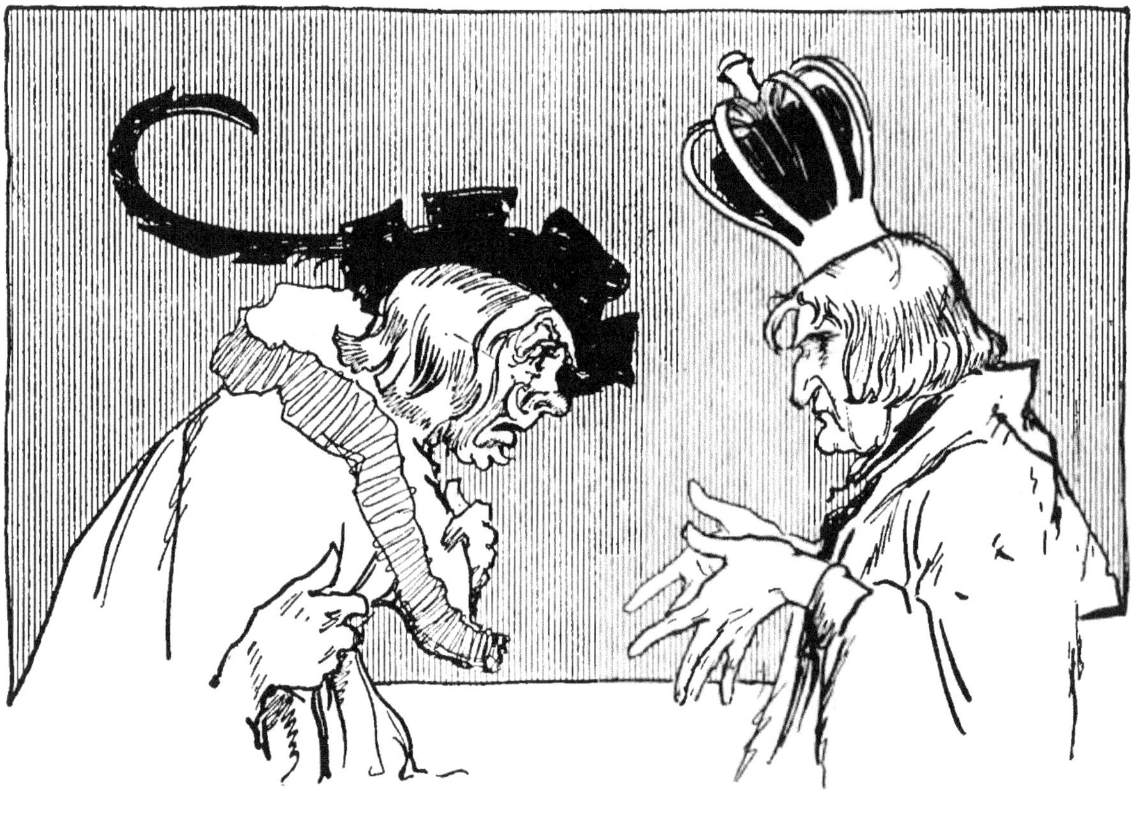

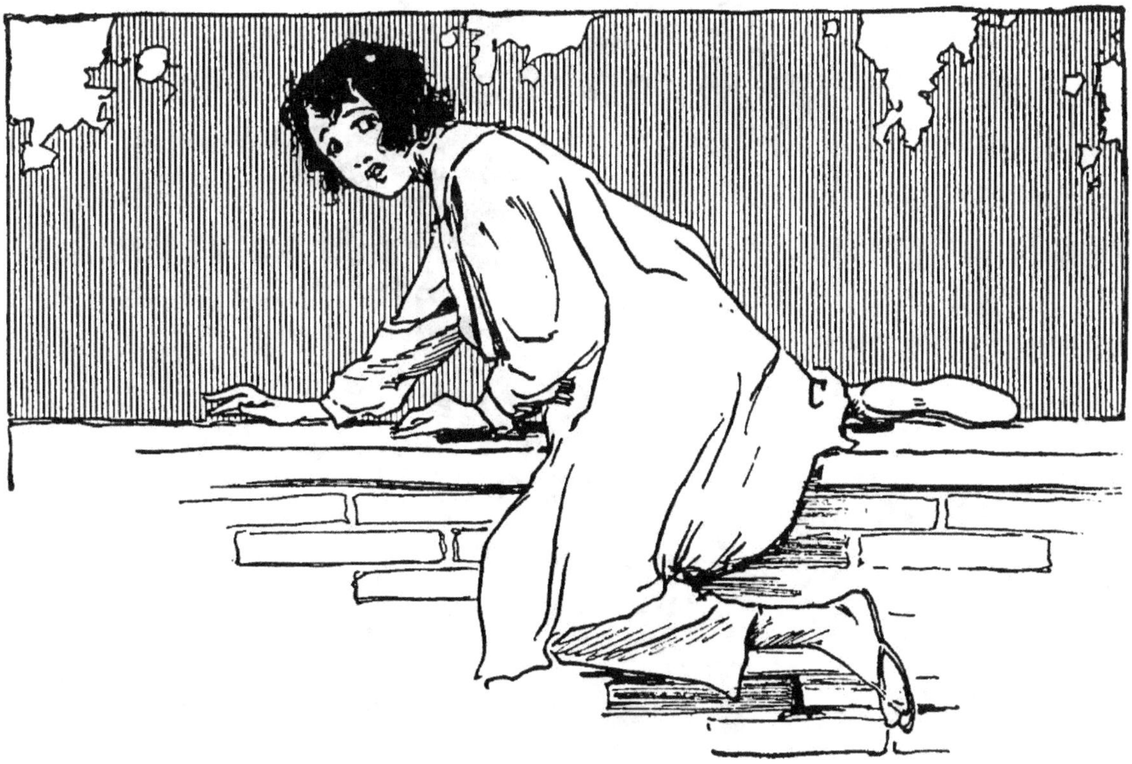

Queen Gloria

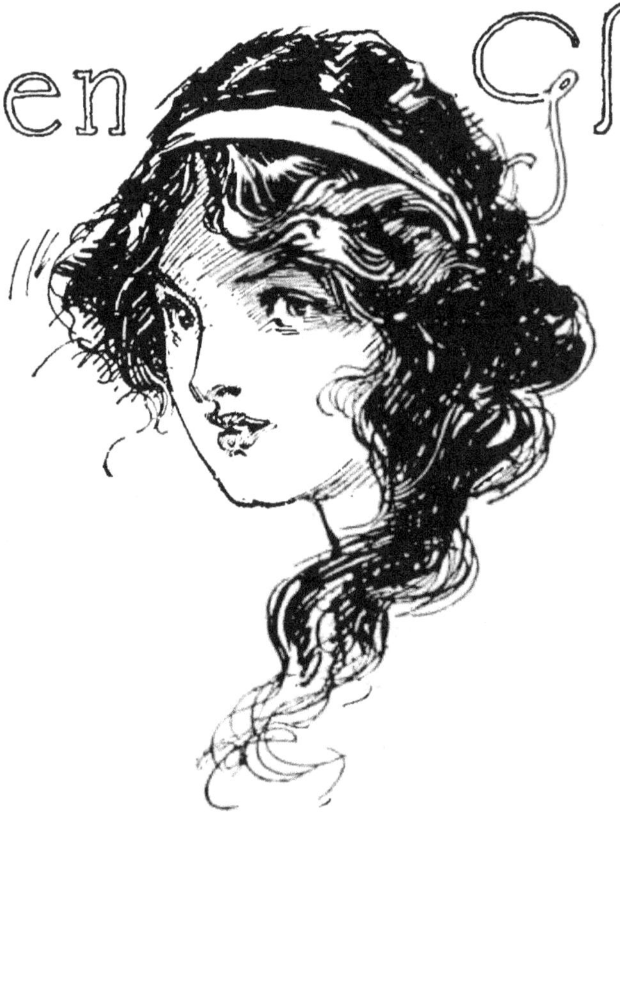

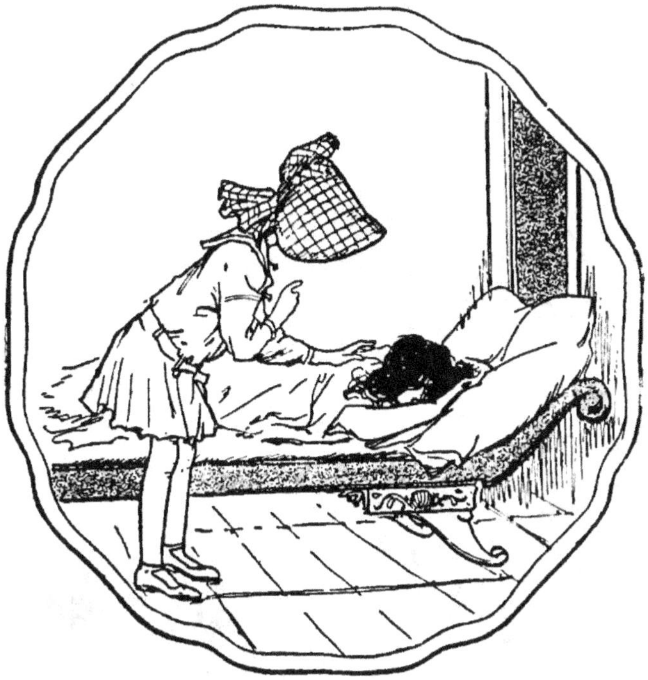

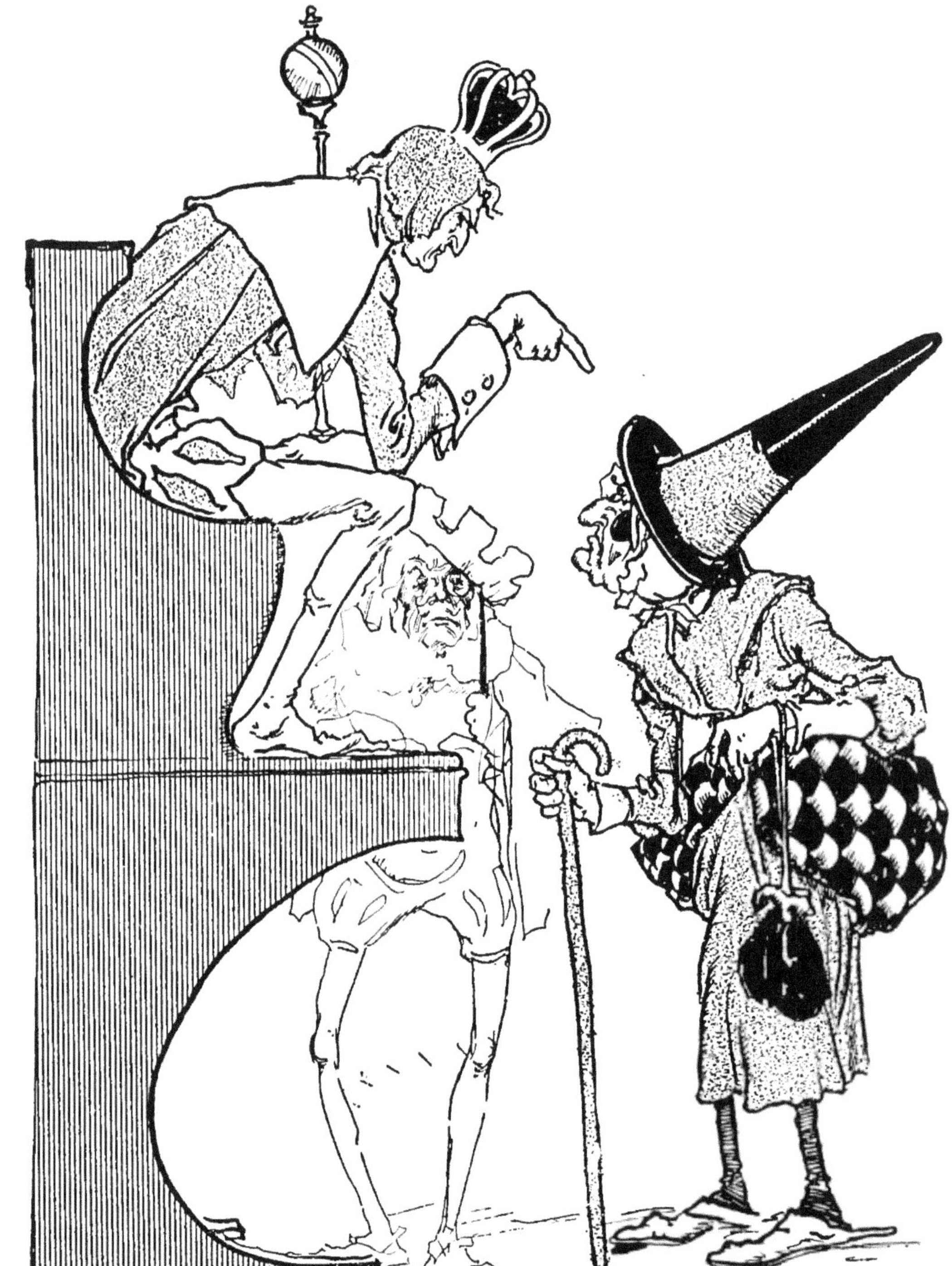

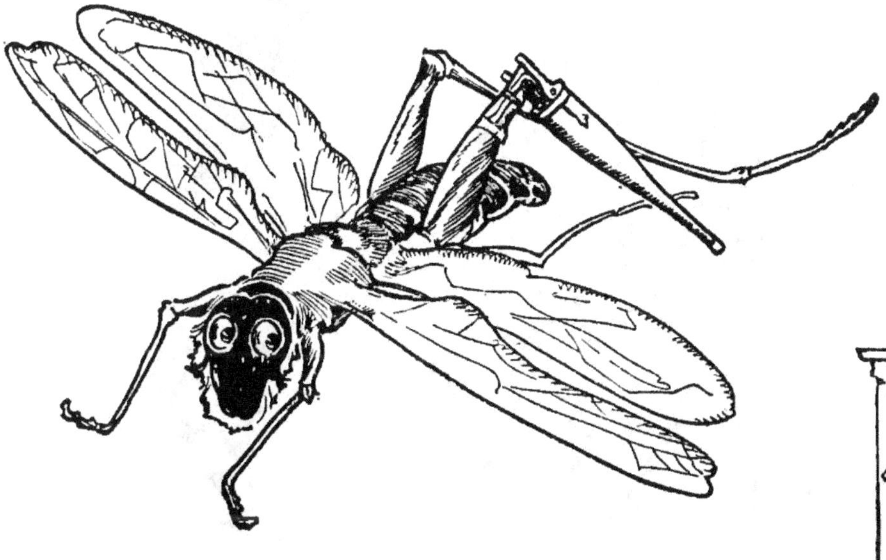

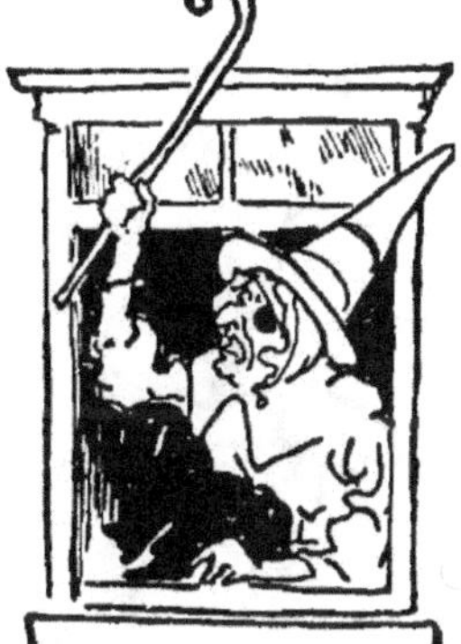

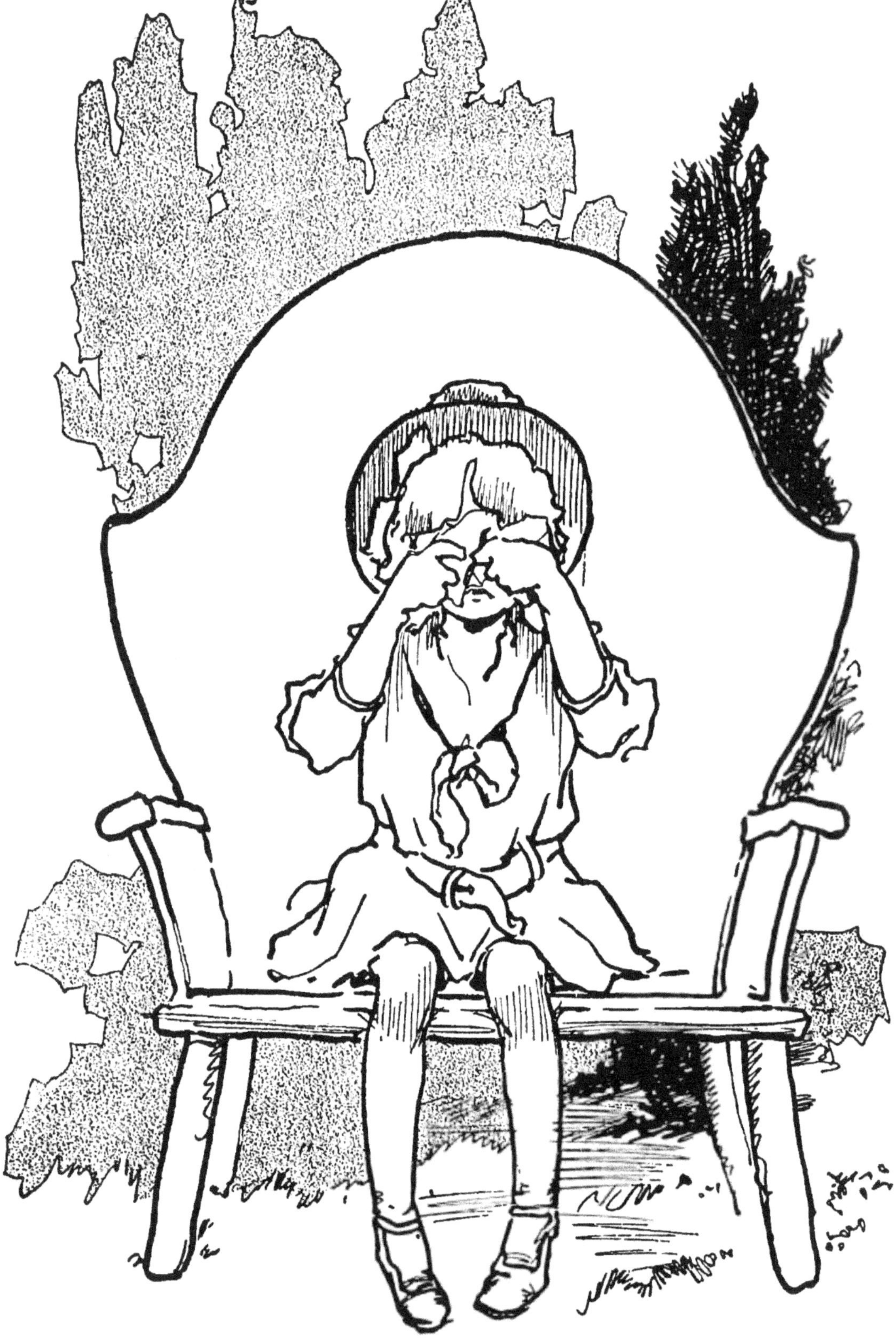

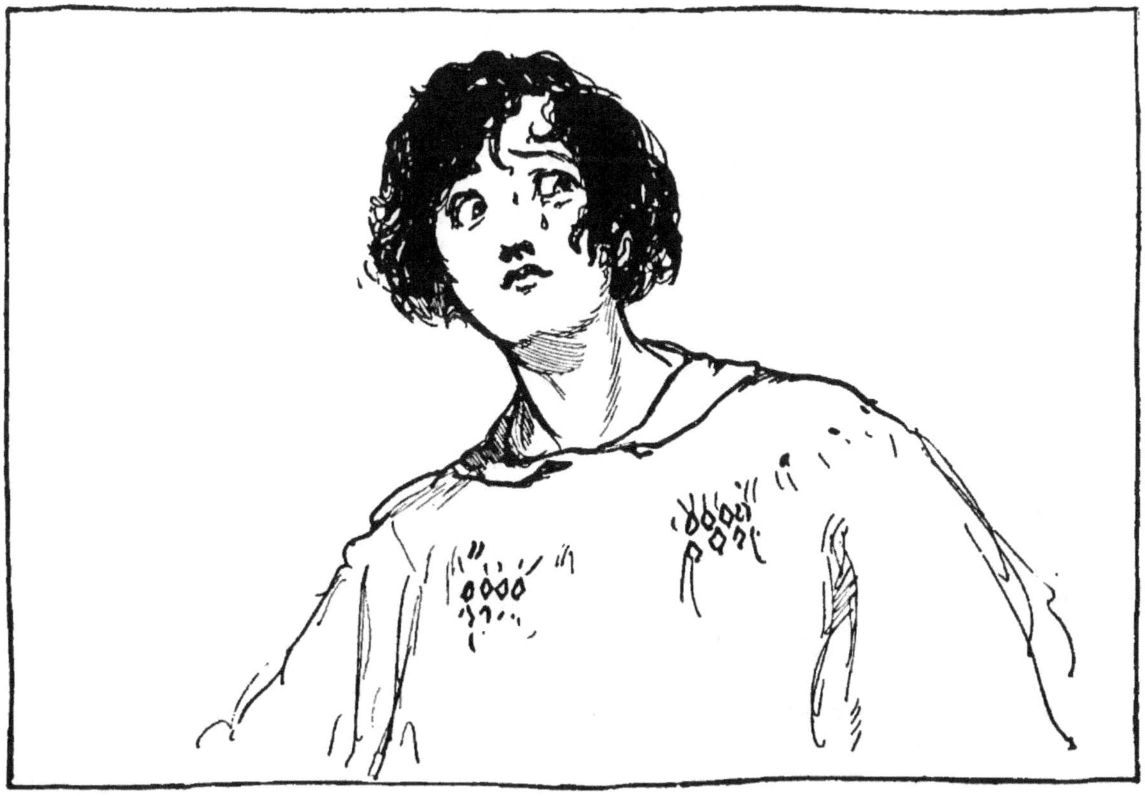

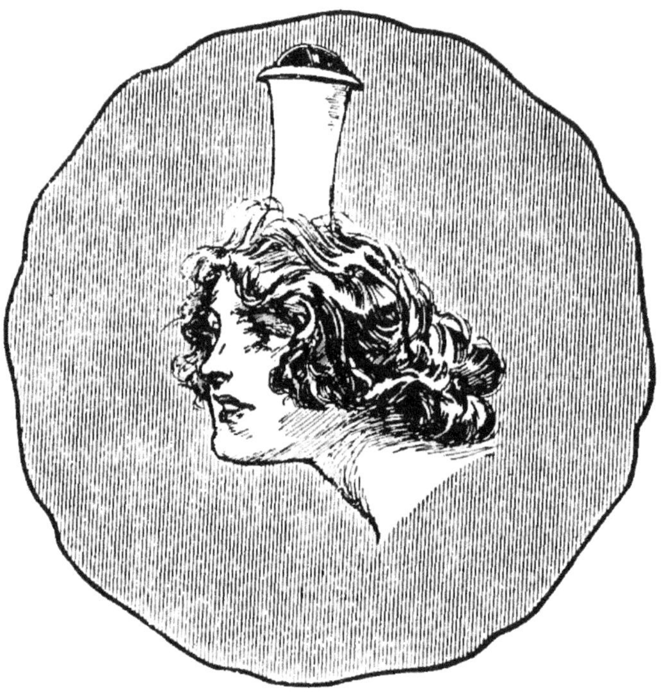

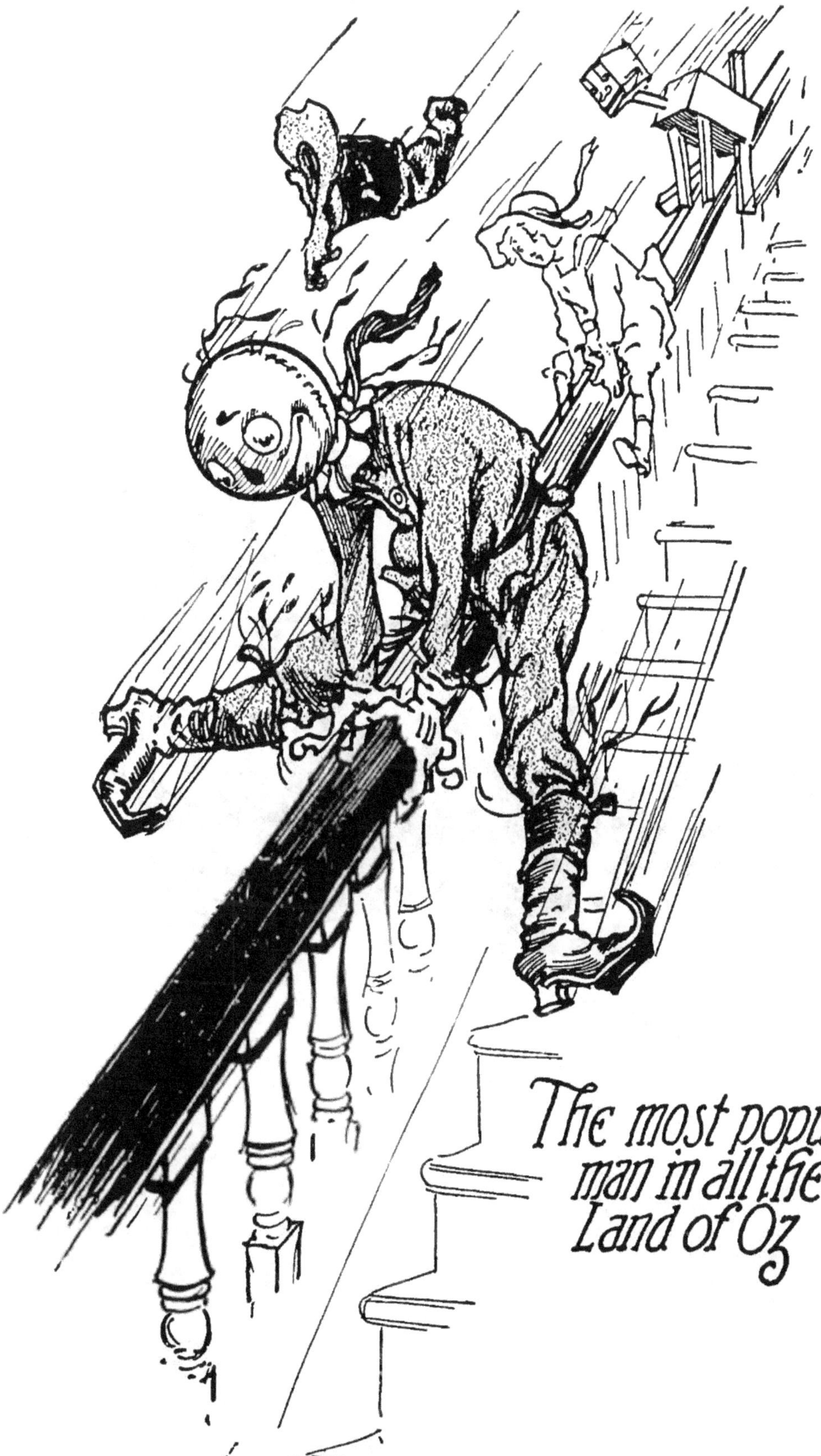

The most popular man in all the Land of Oz

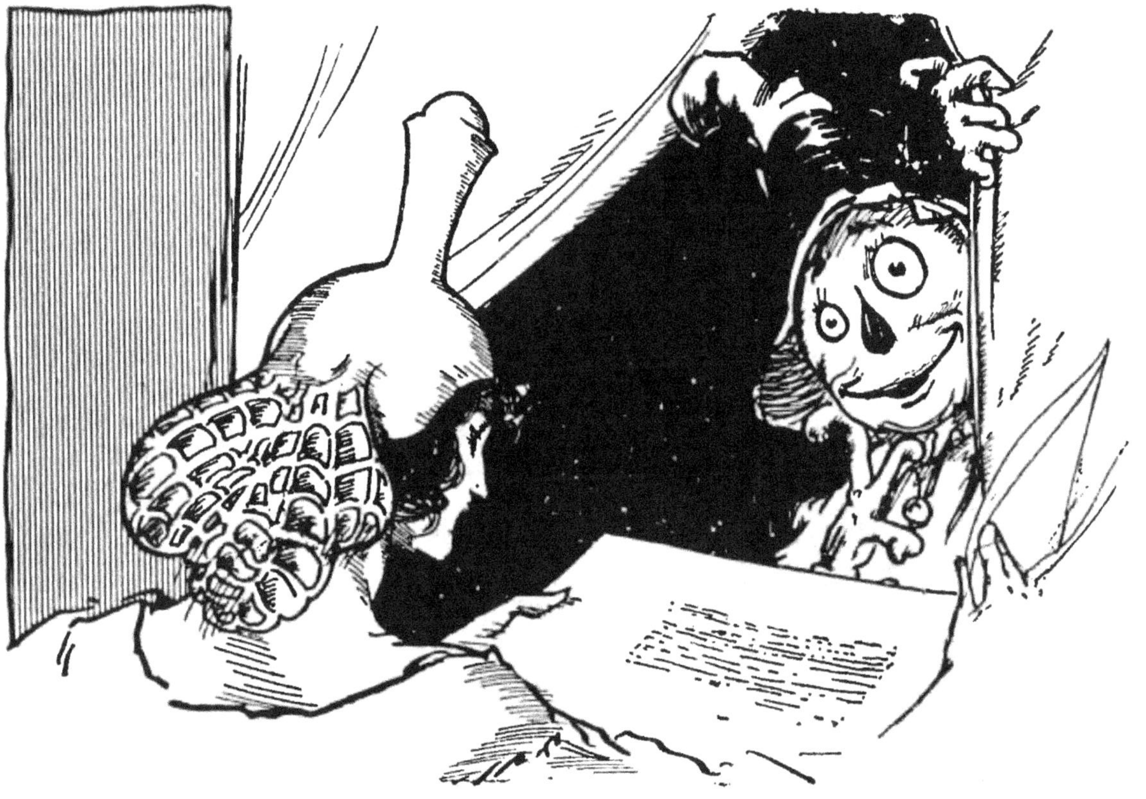

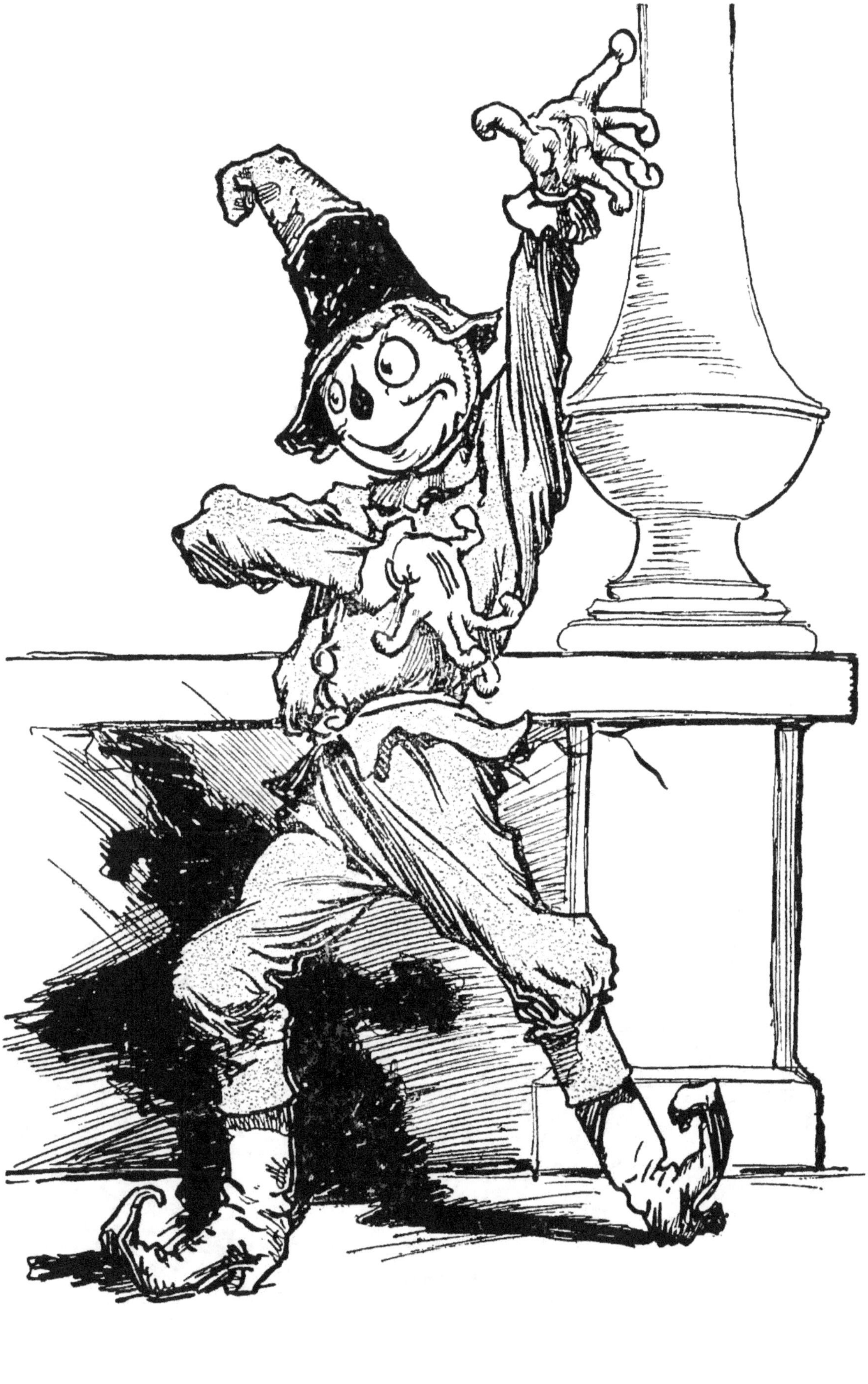

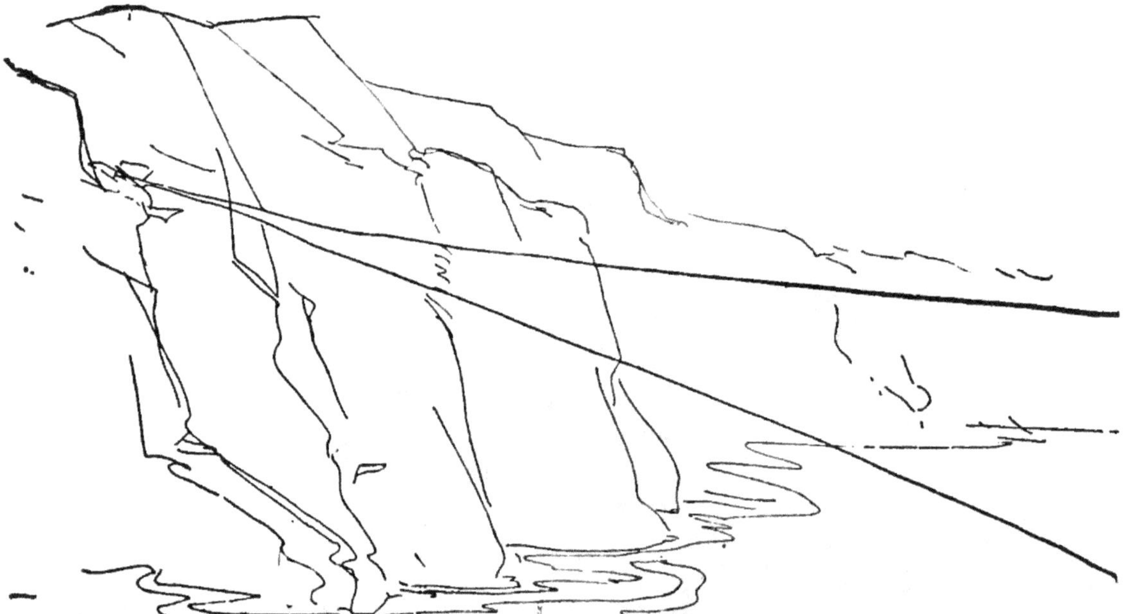

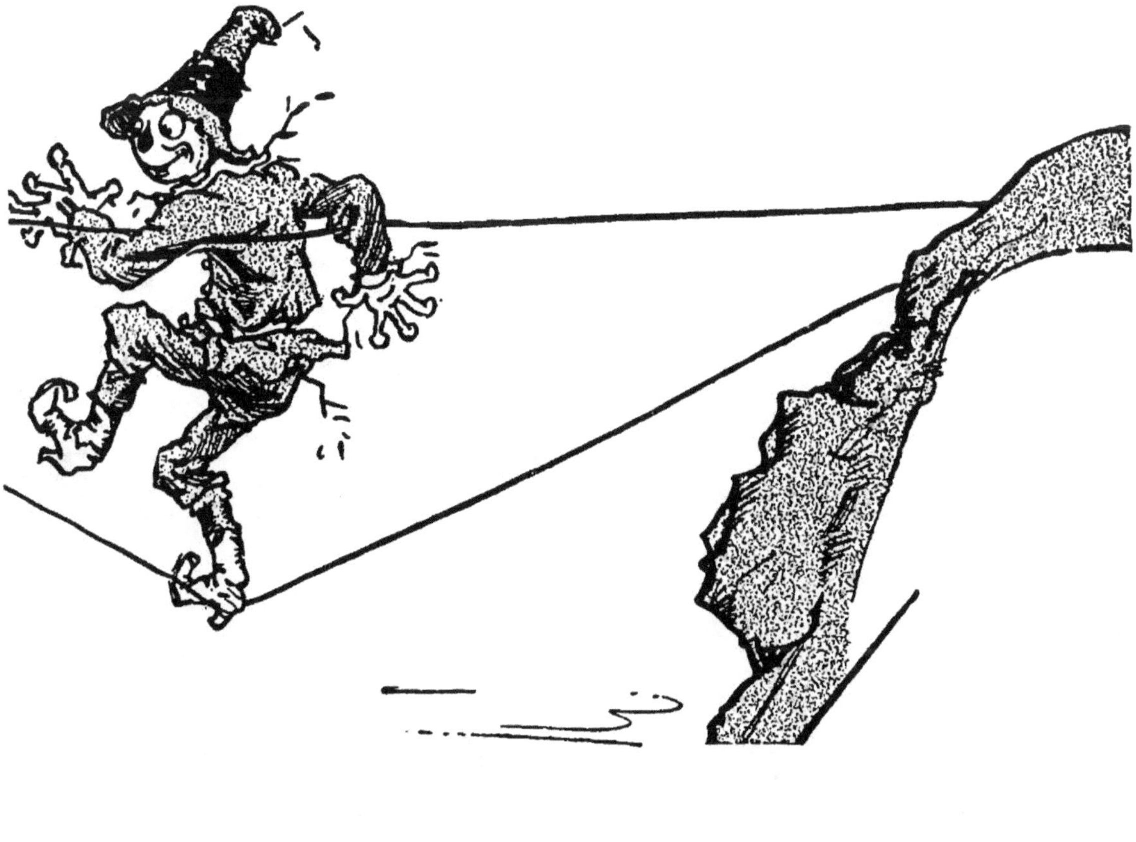

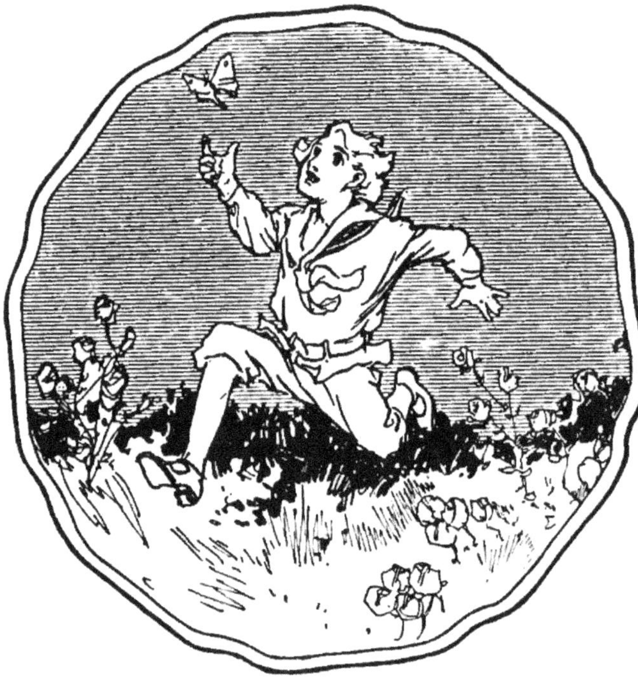

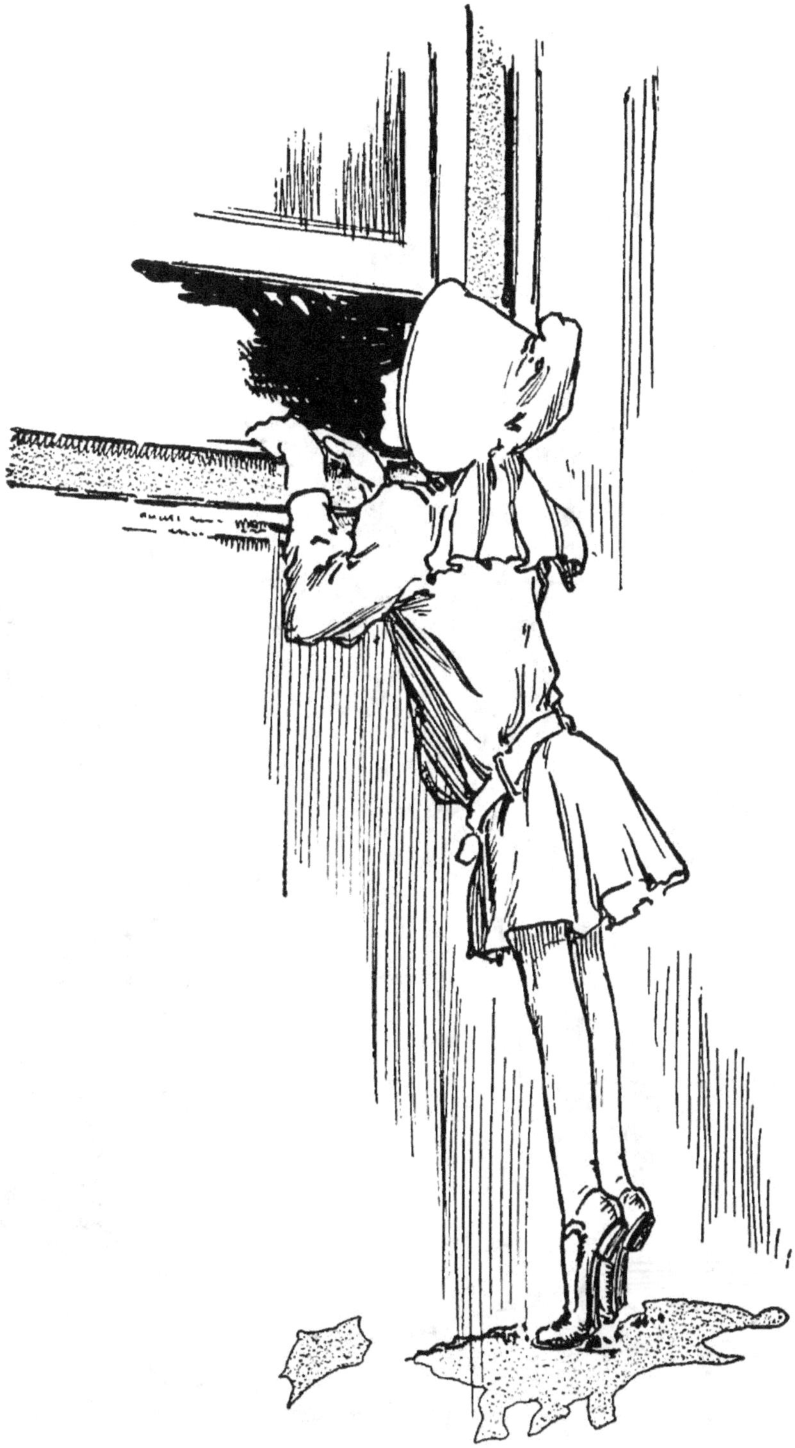

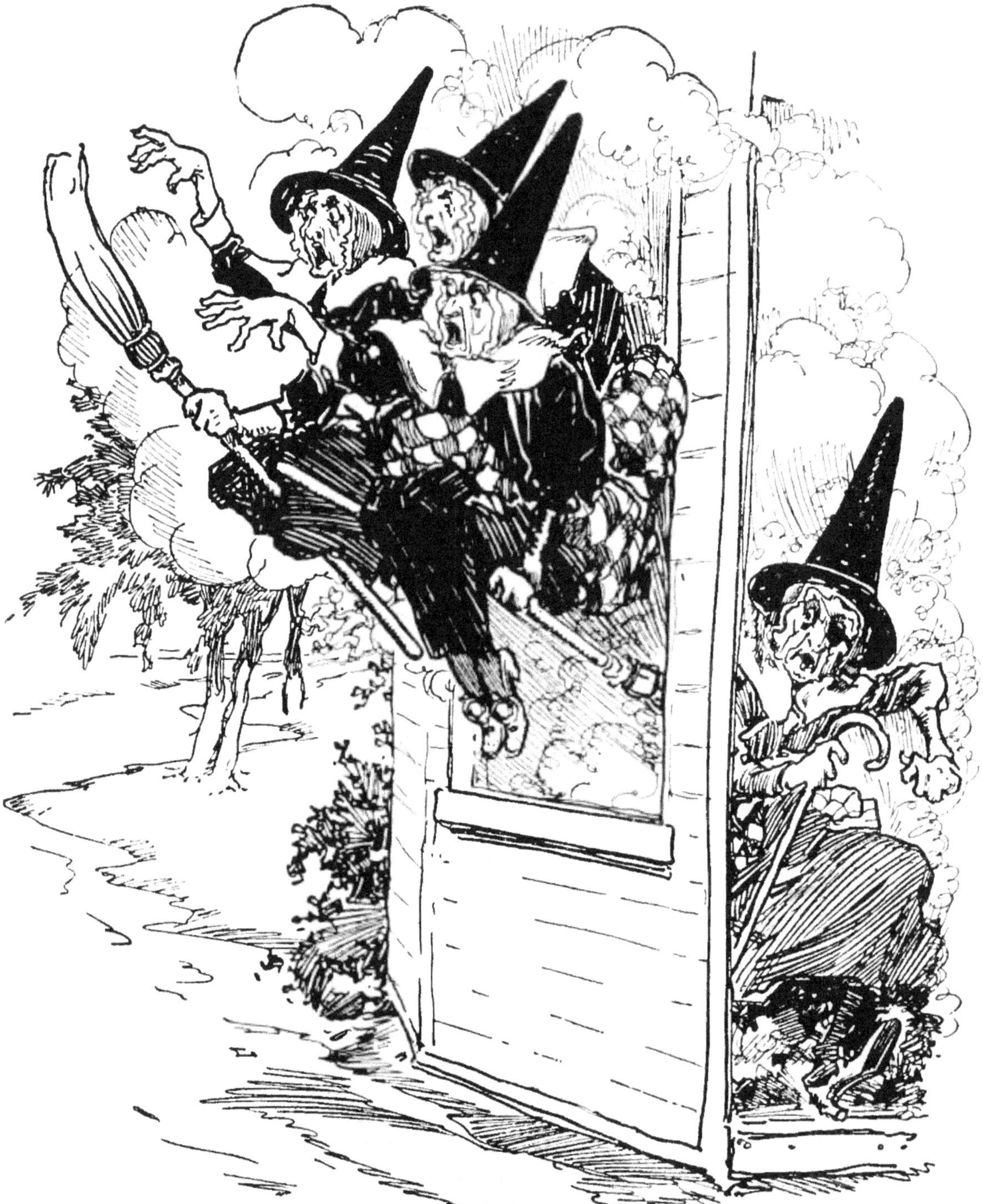

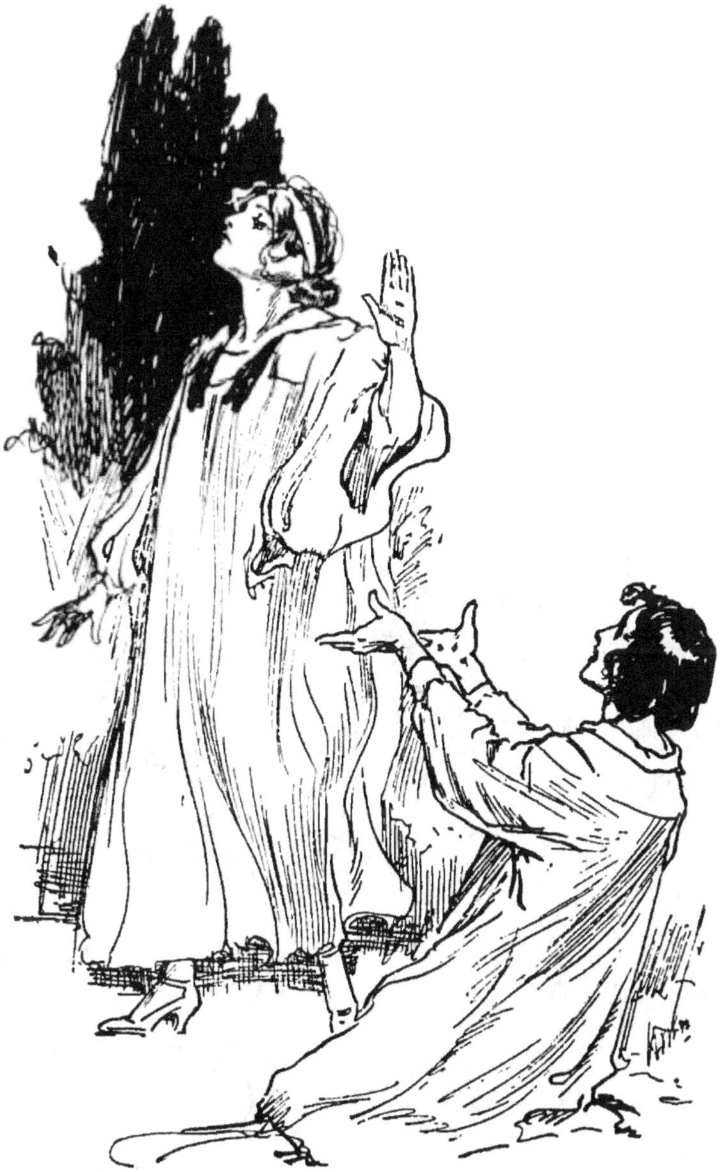

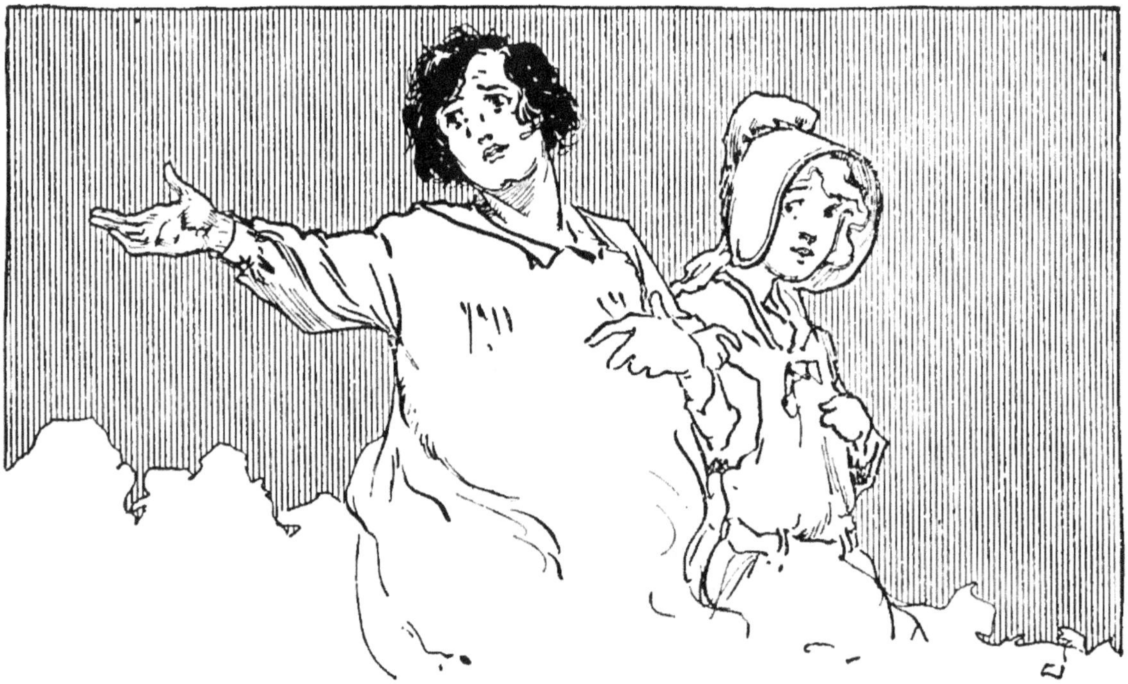

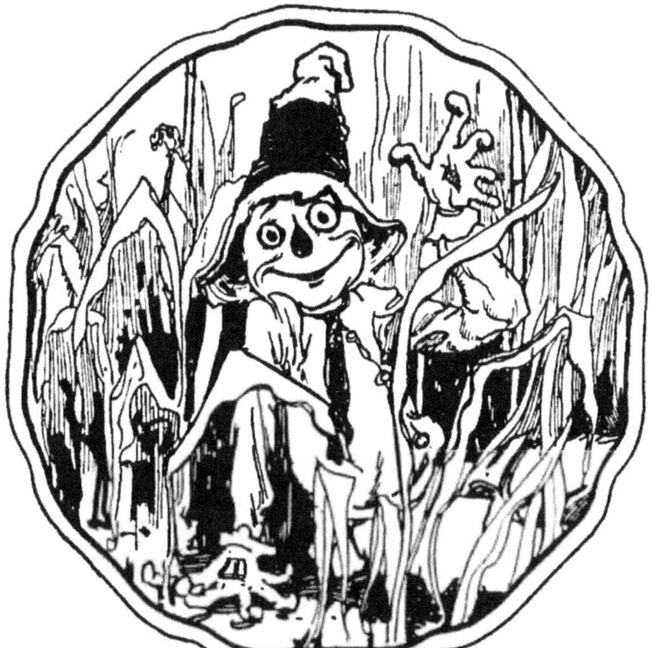

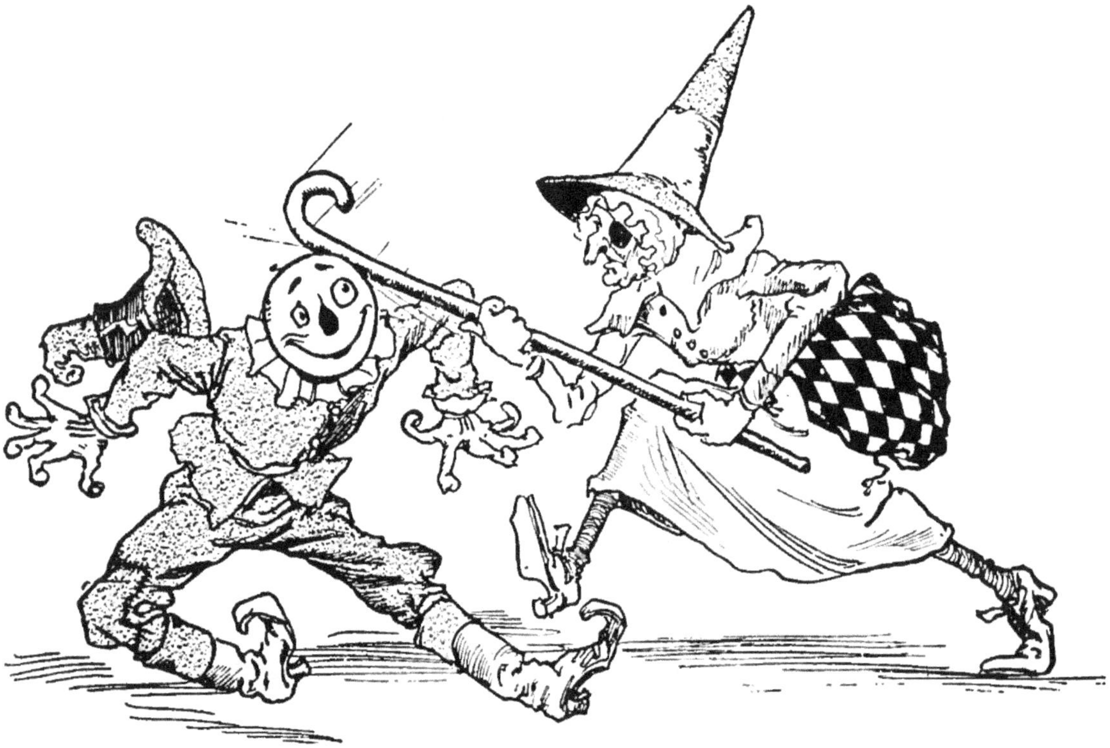

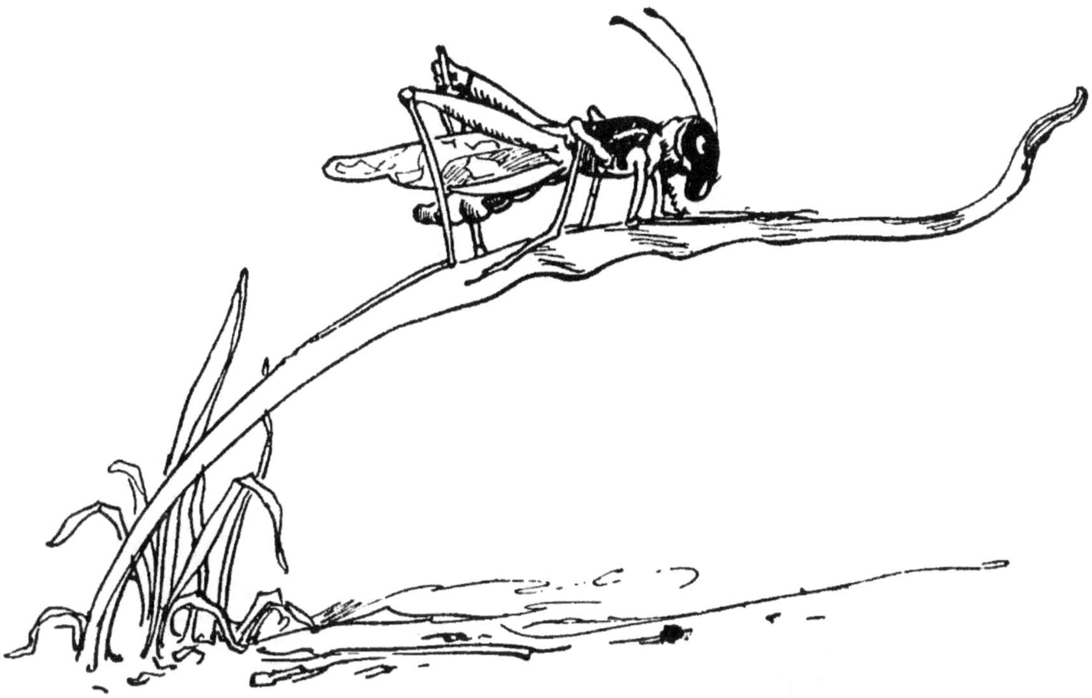

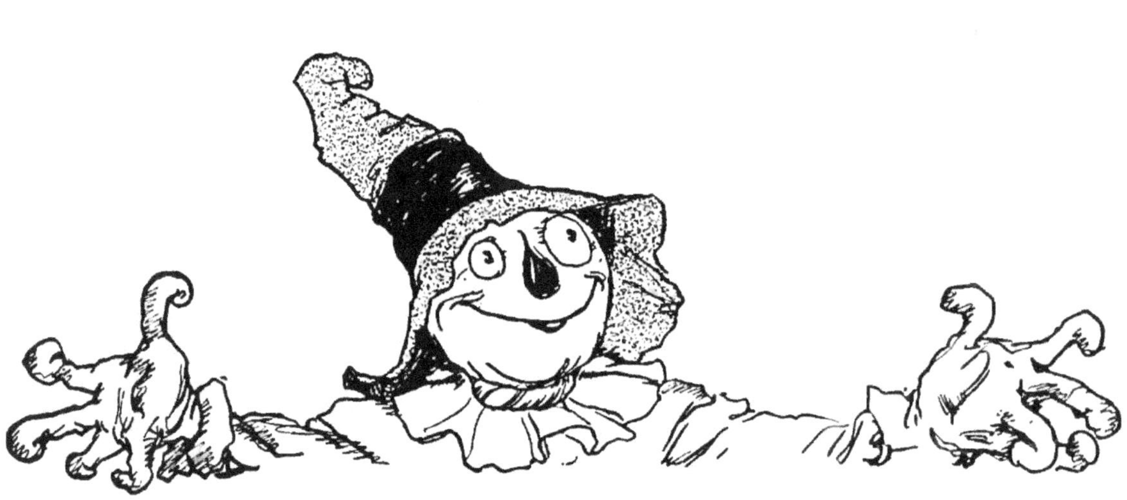

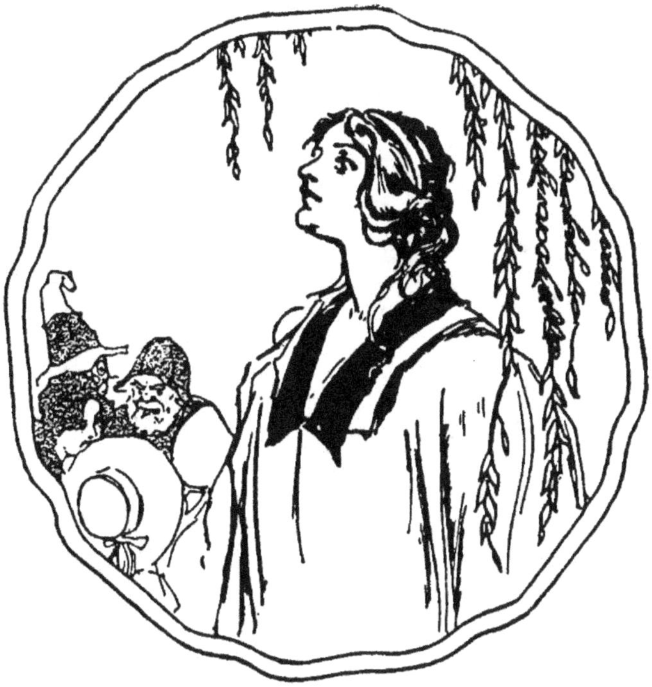

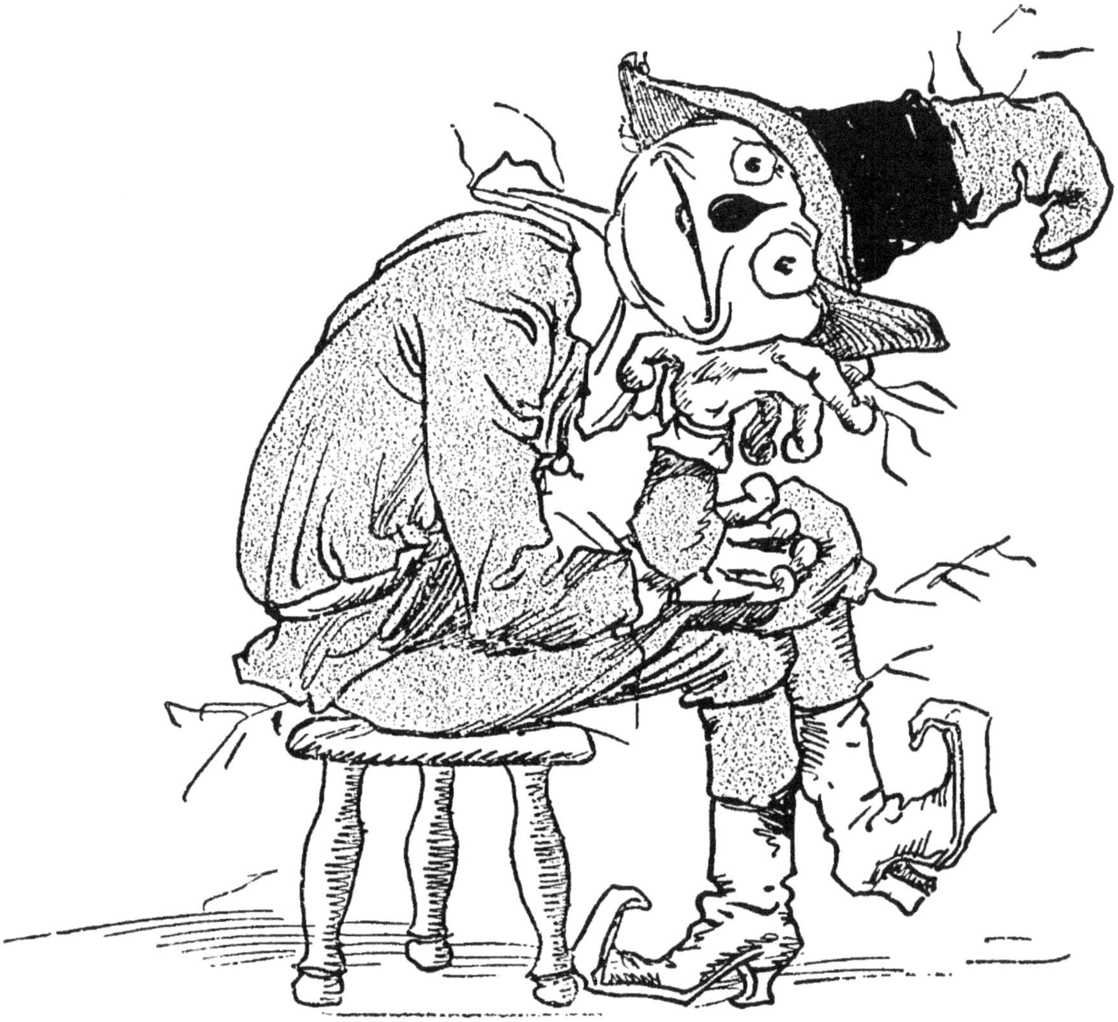

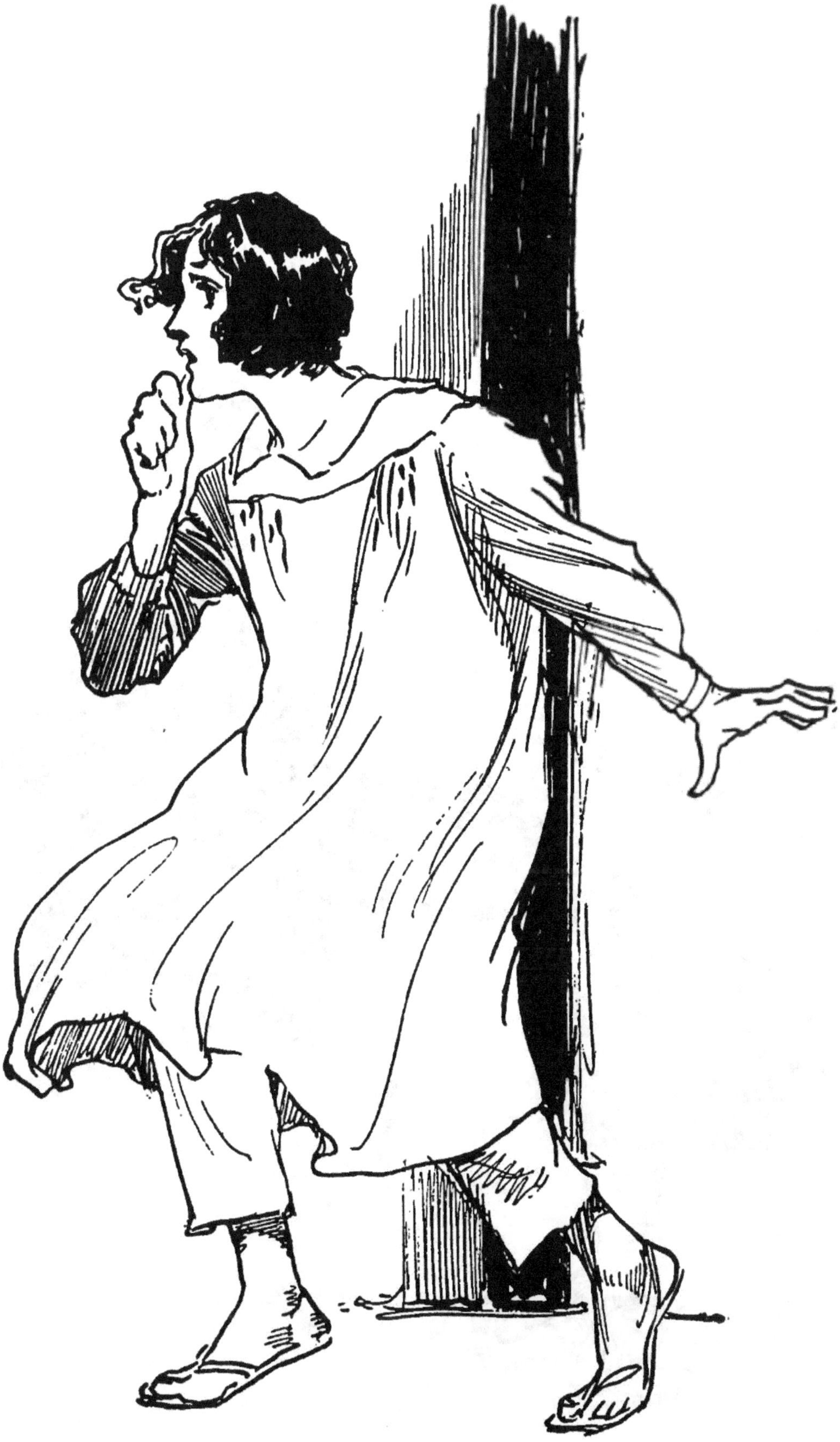

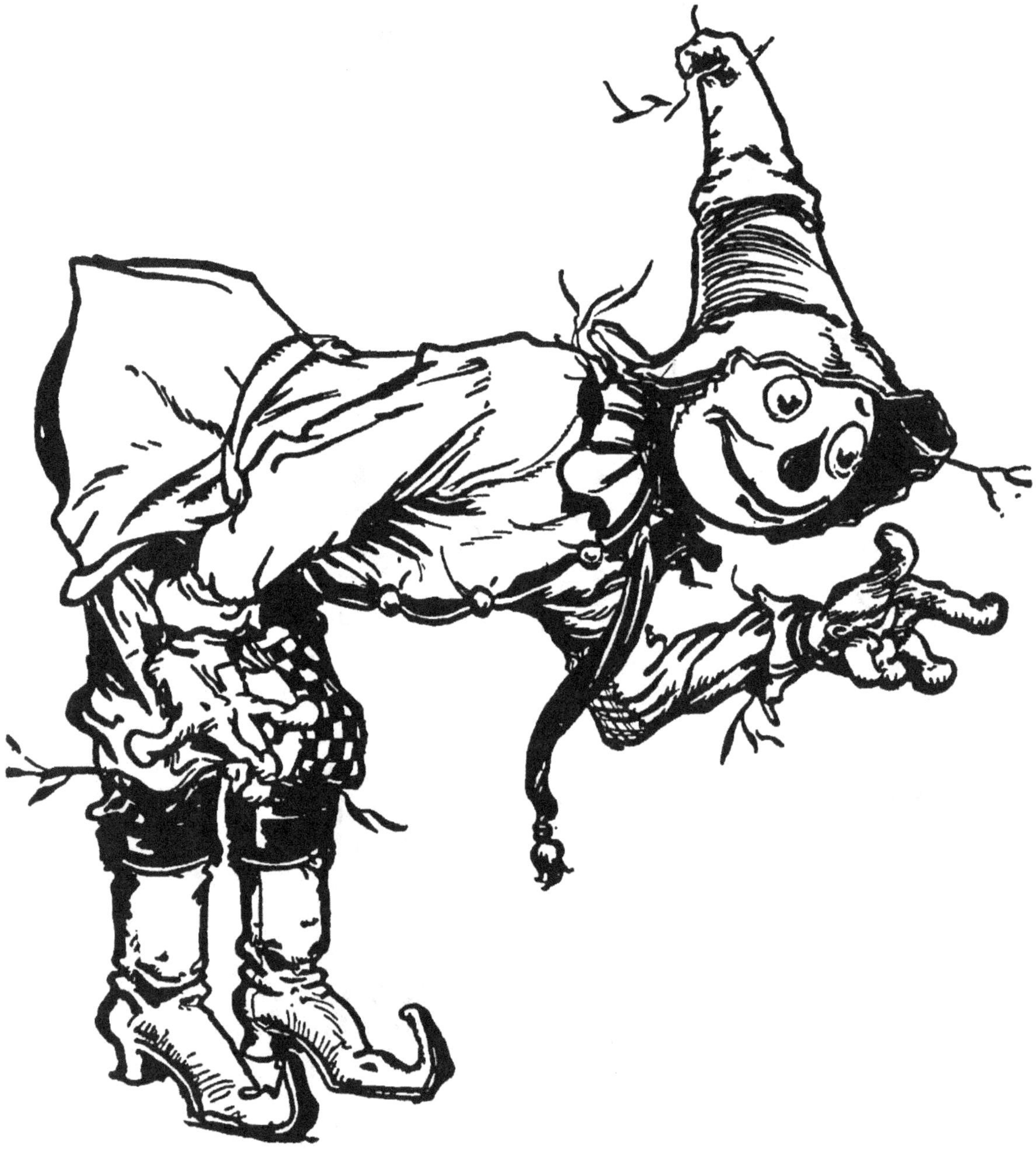

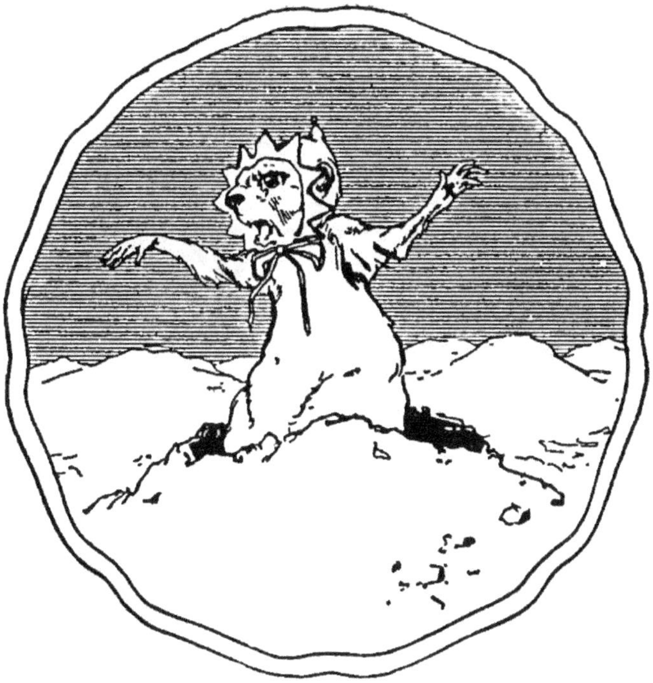

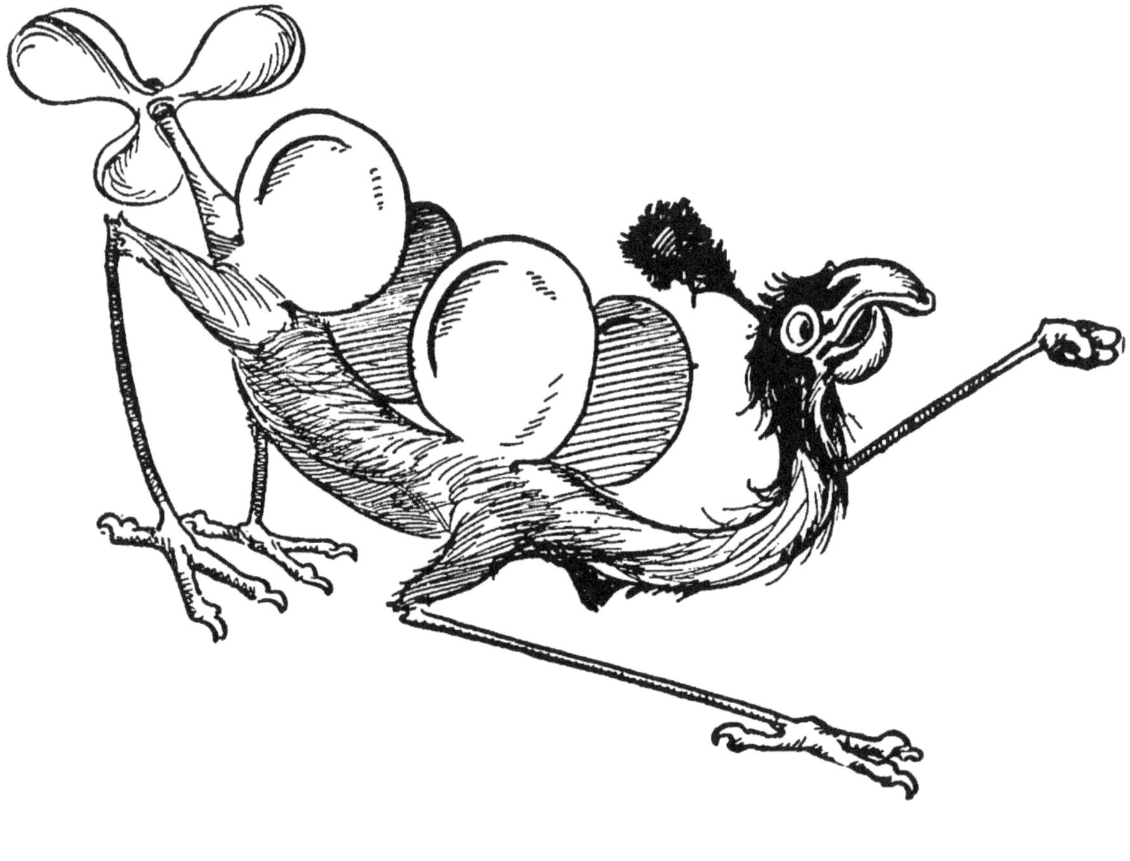

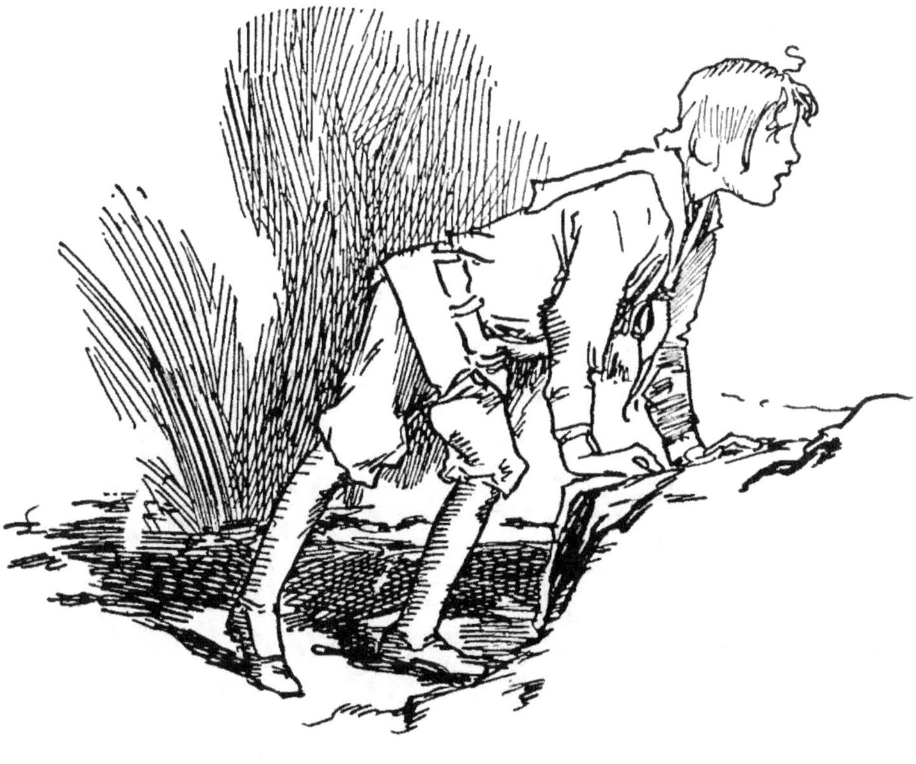

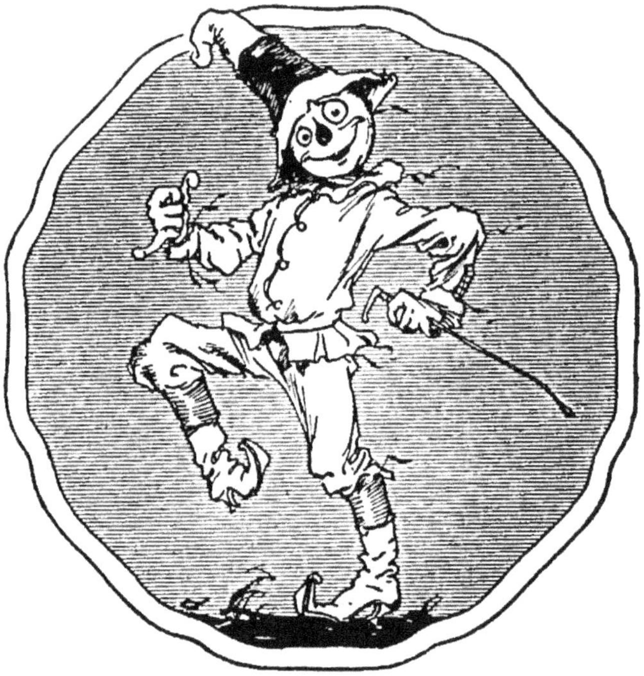

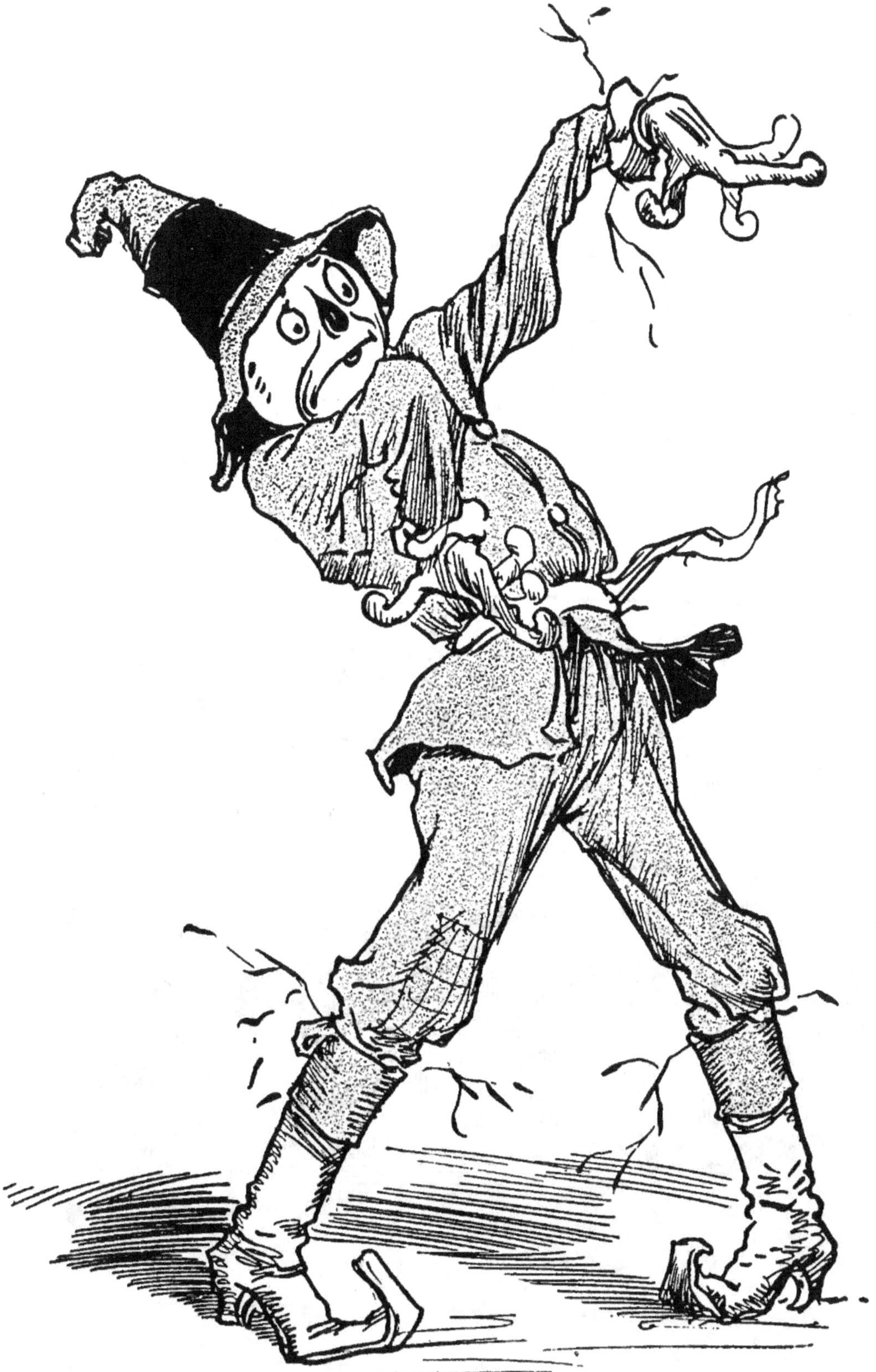

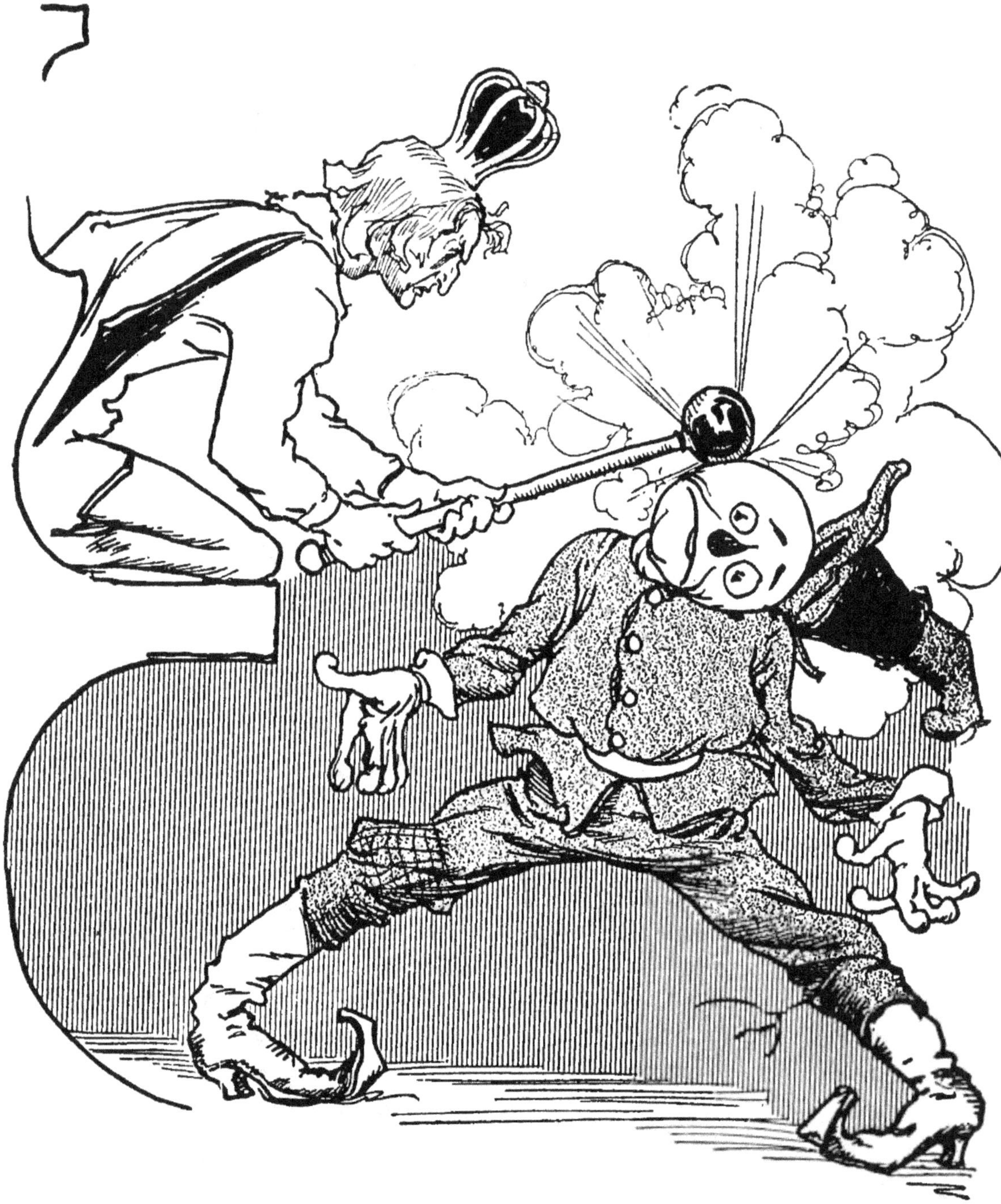

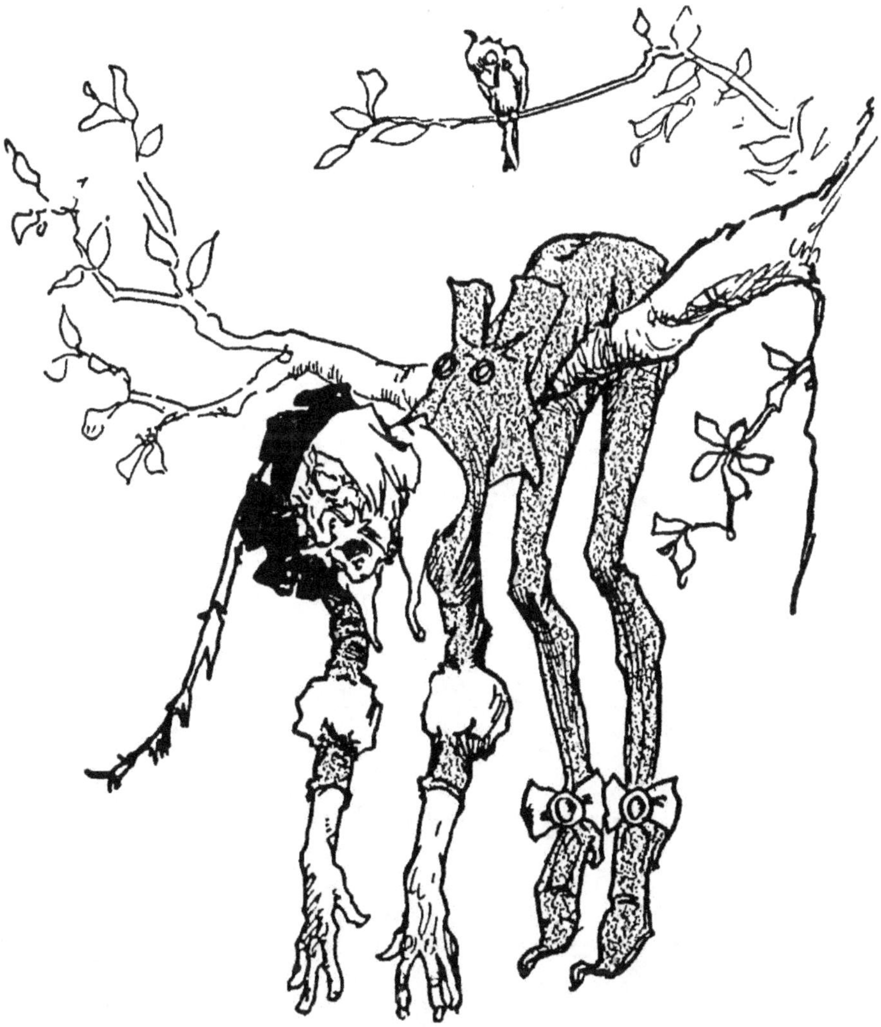

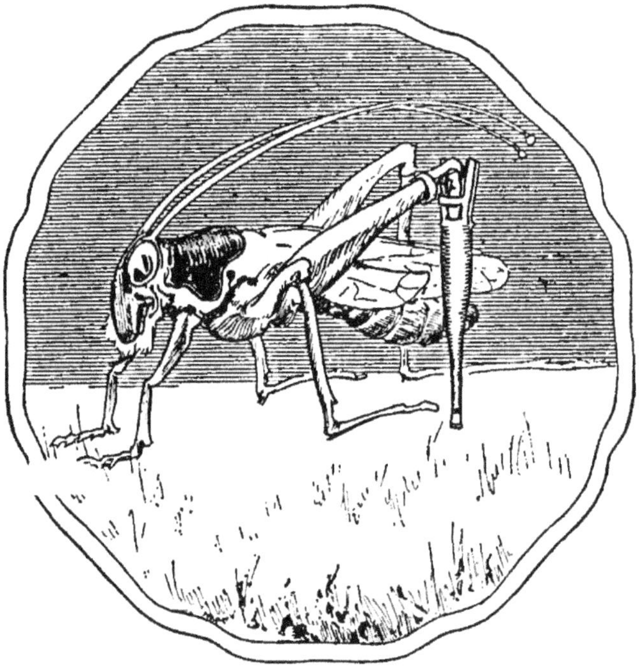

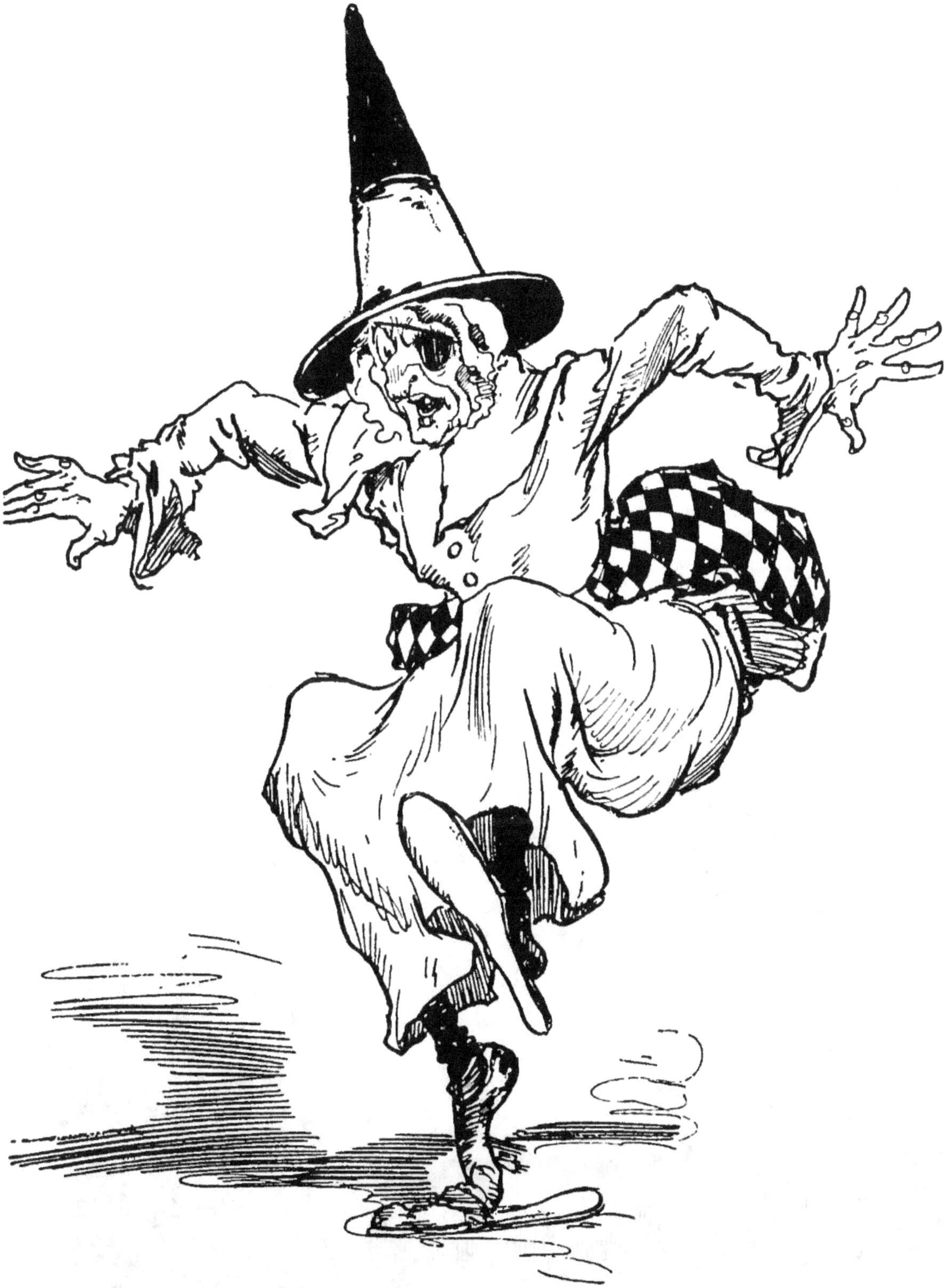

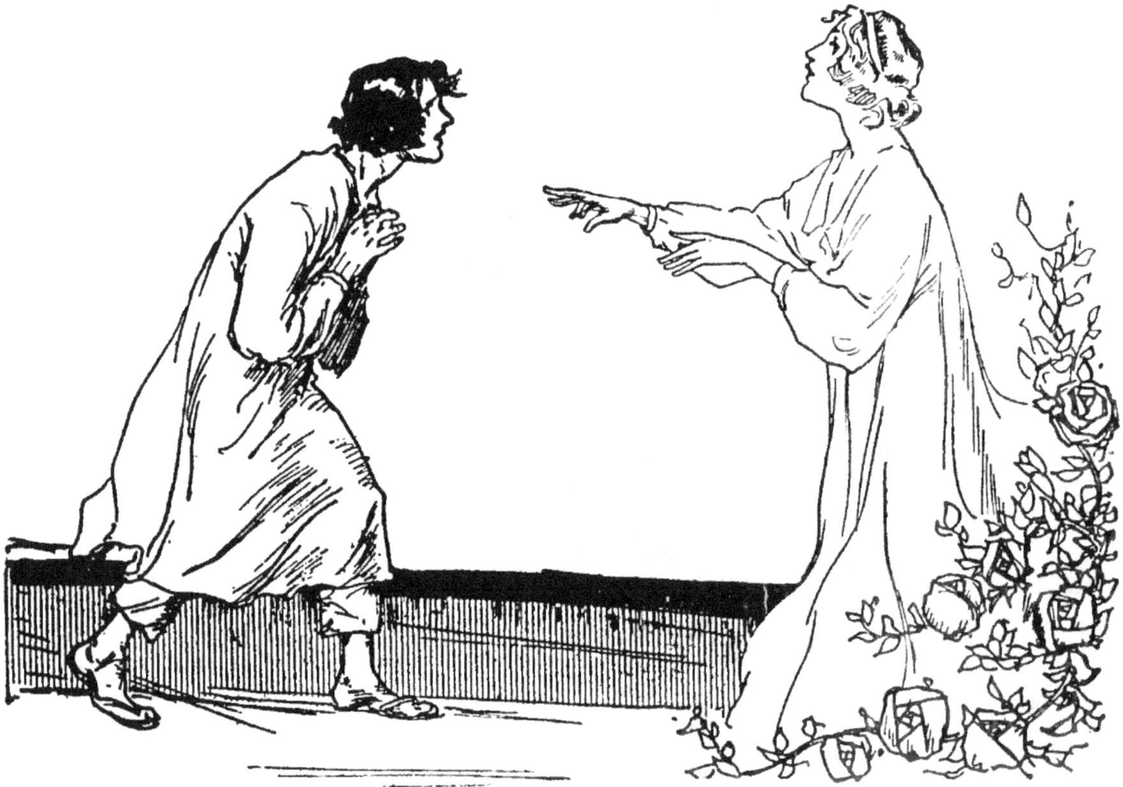

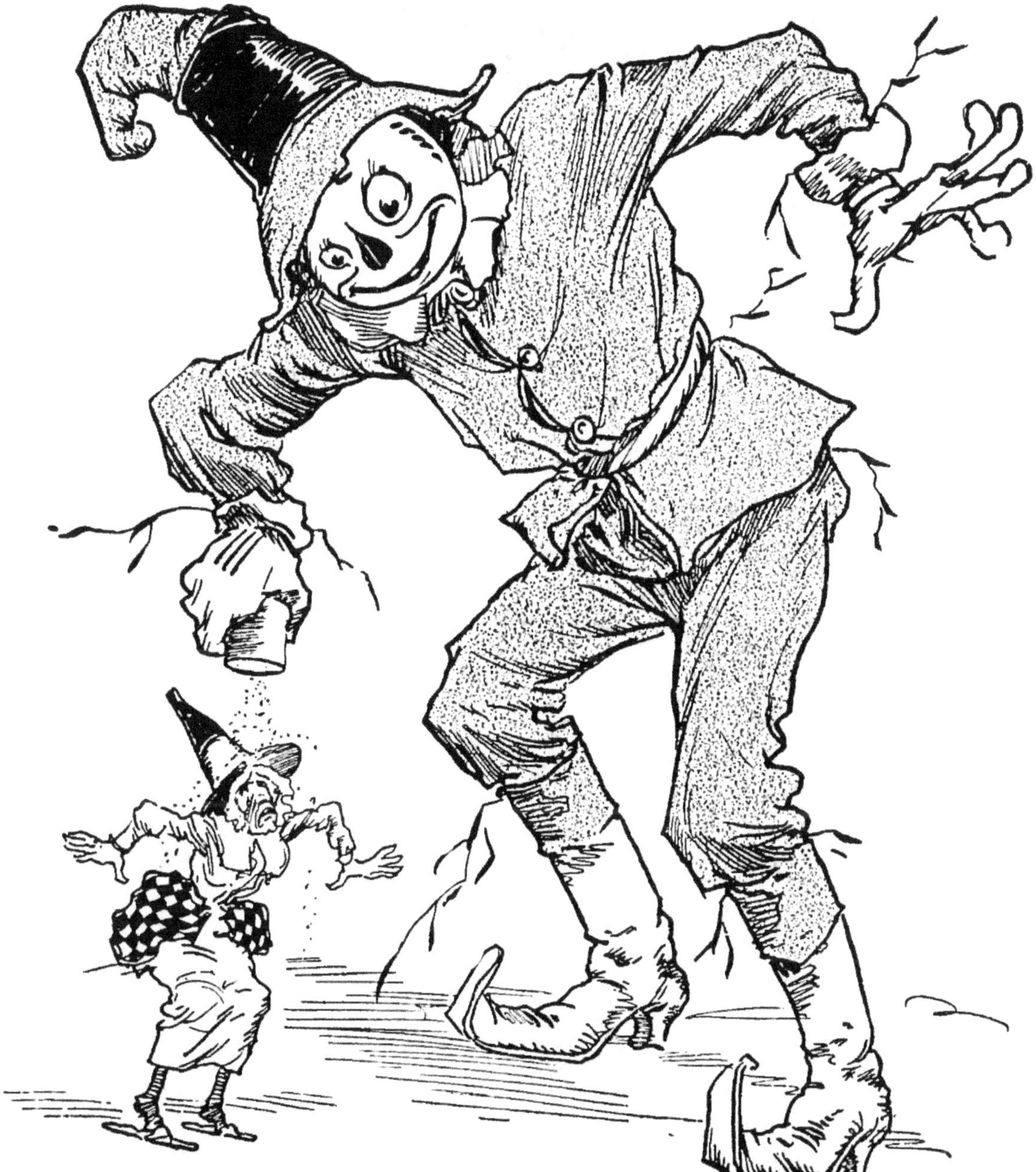

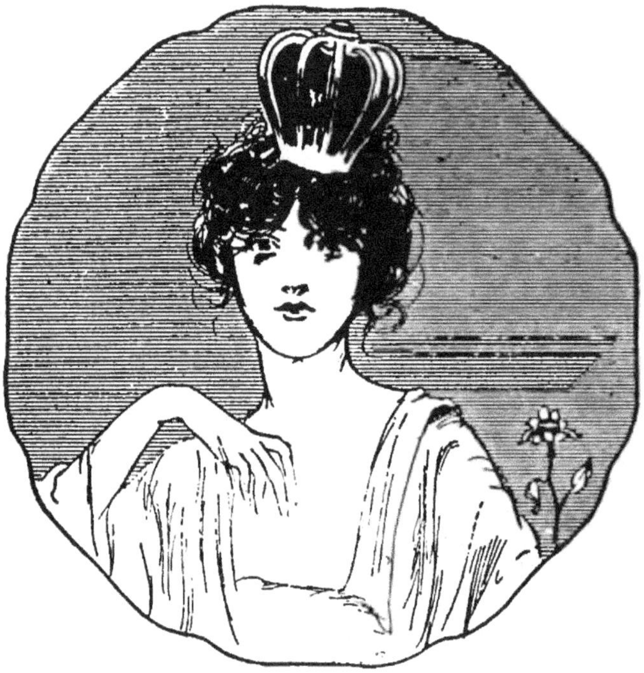

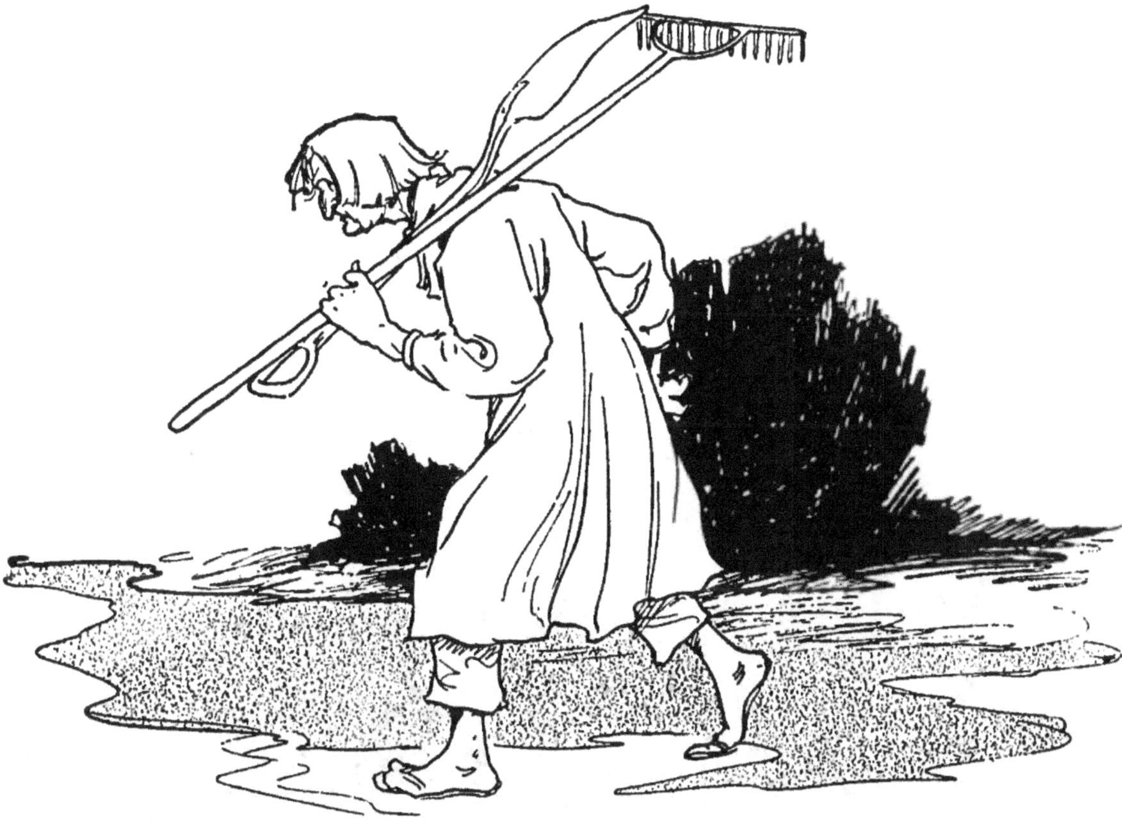

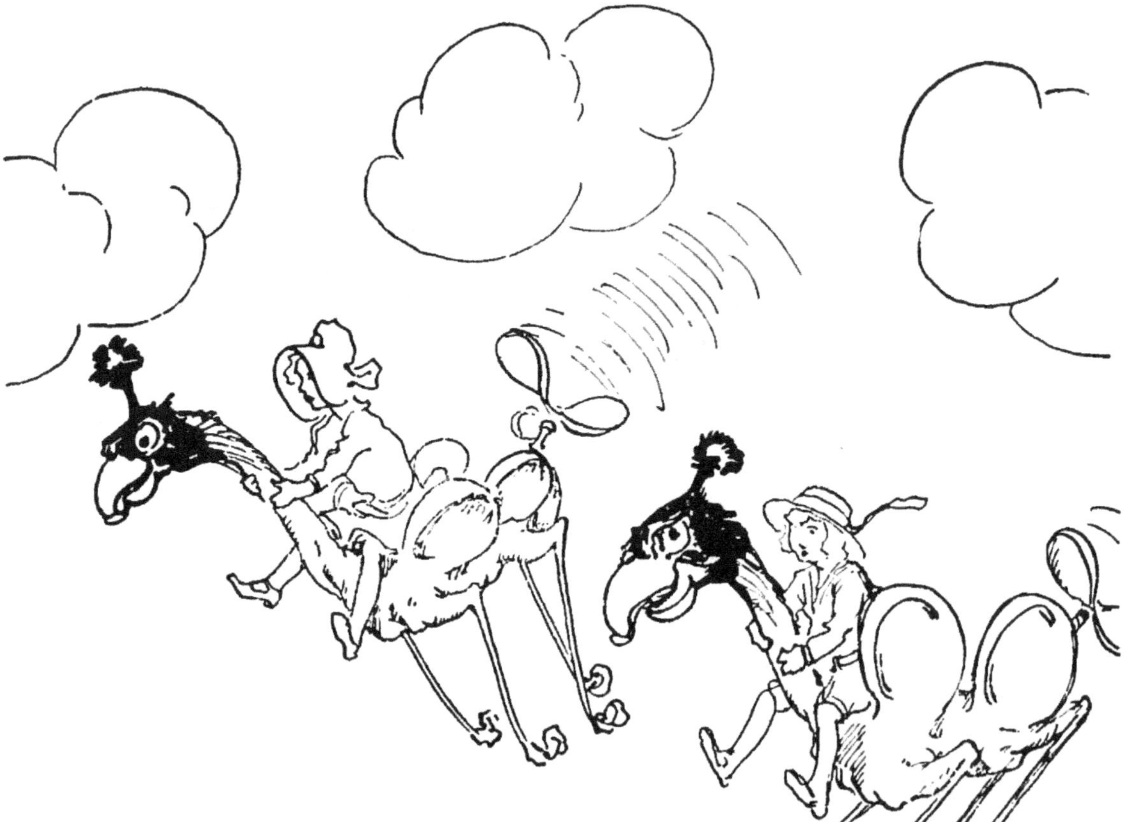

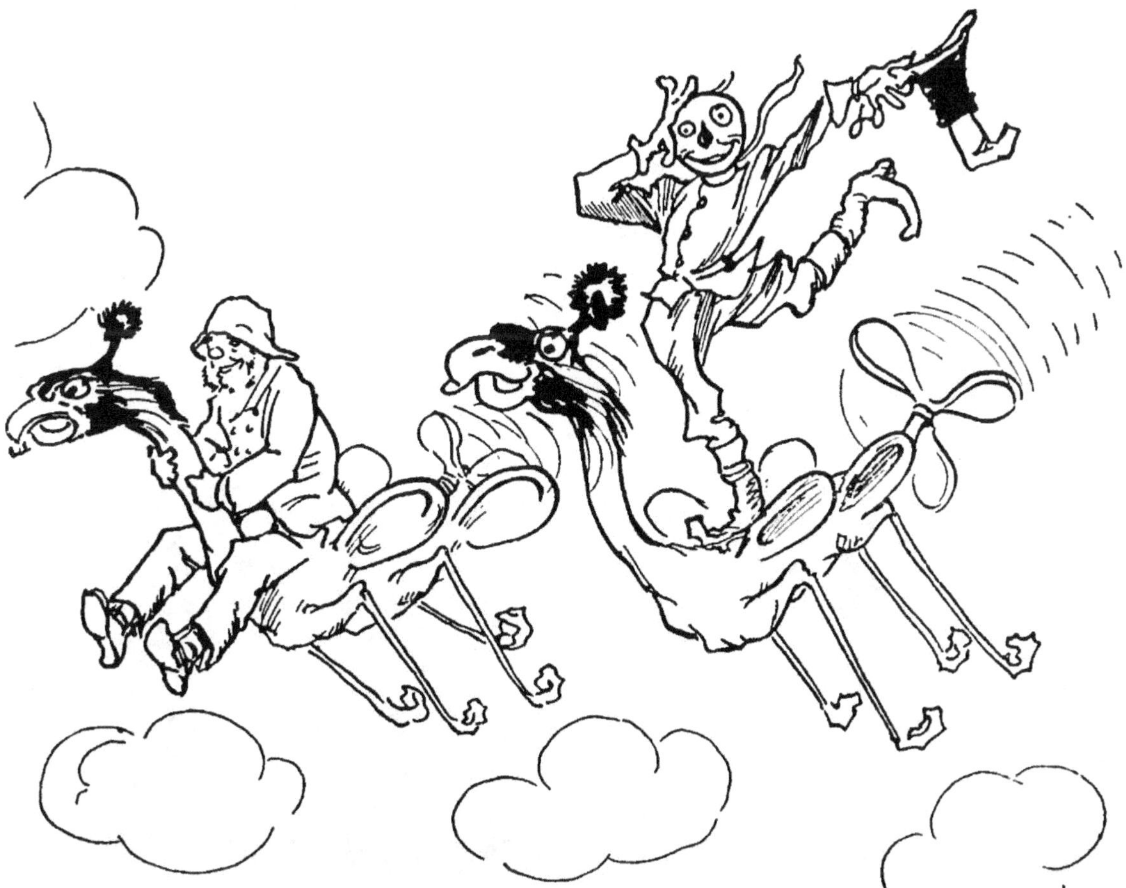

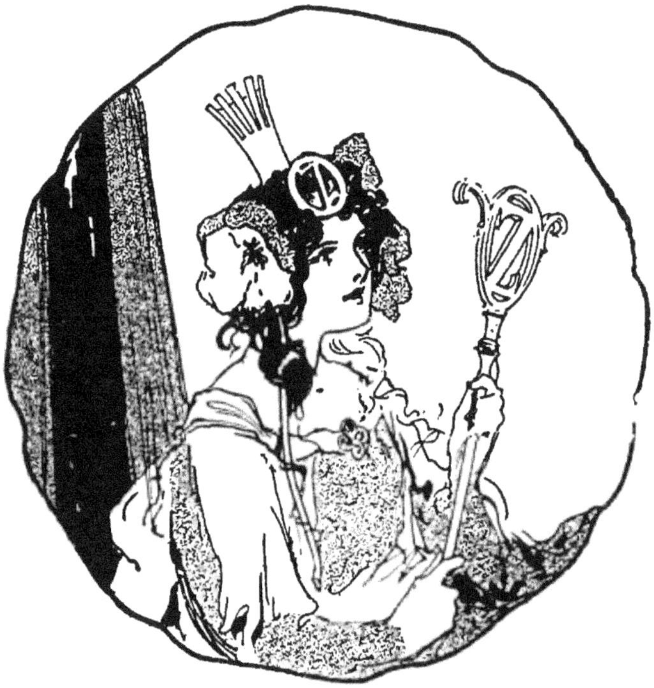

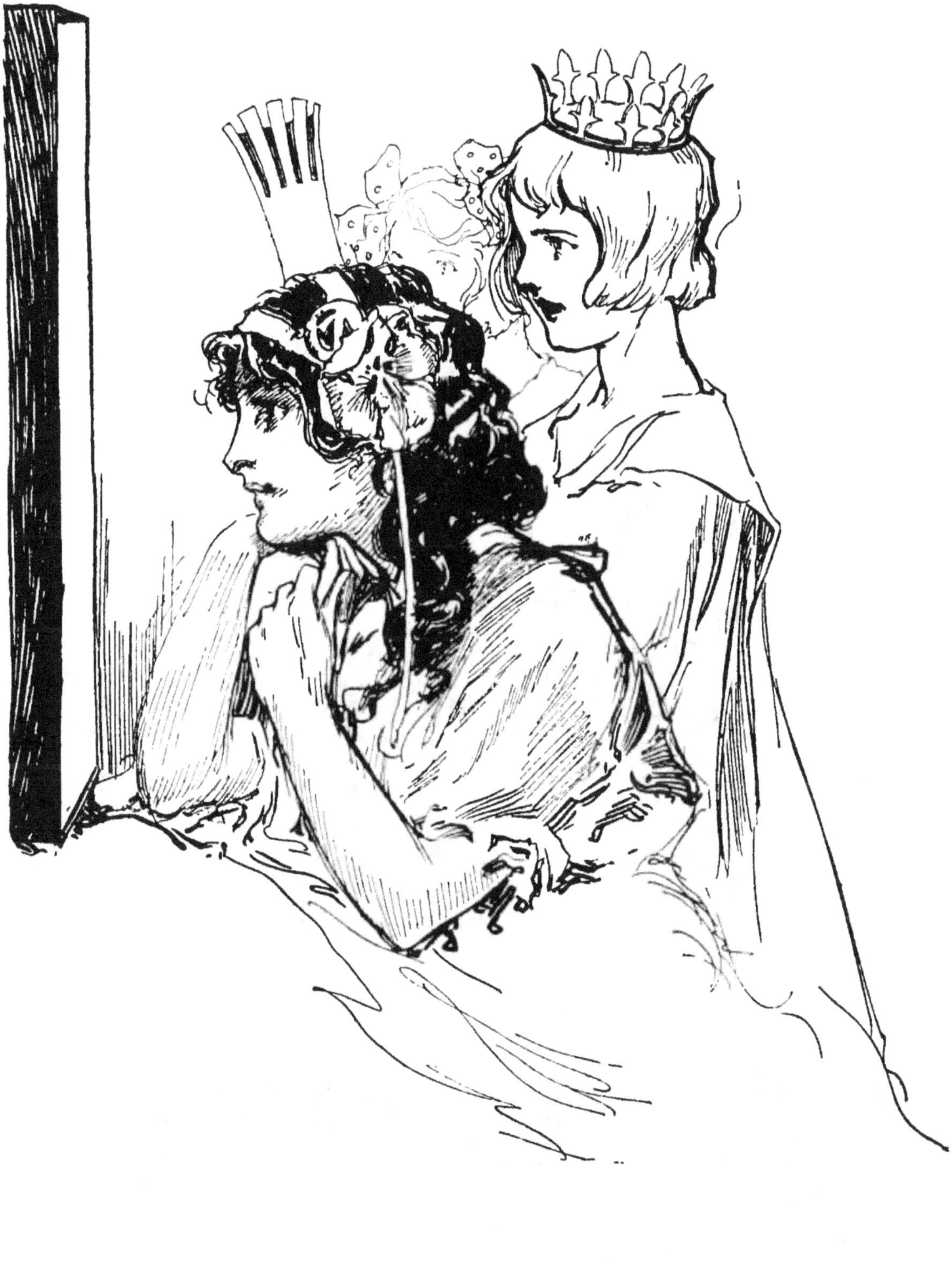

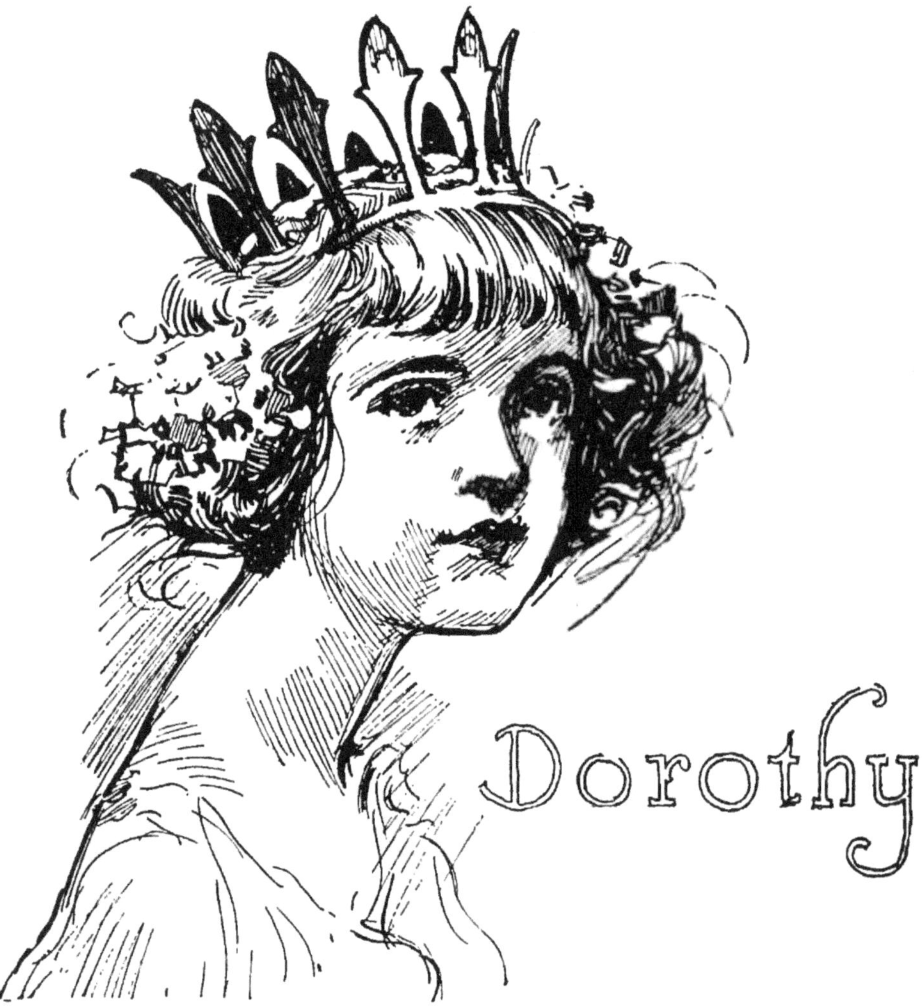
Dorothy

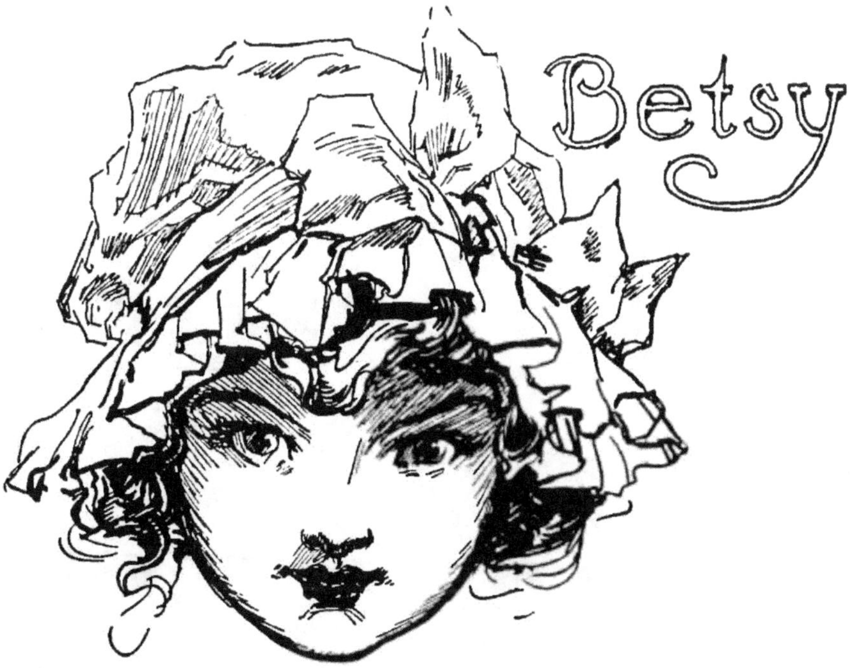
Betsy

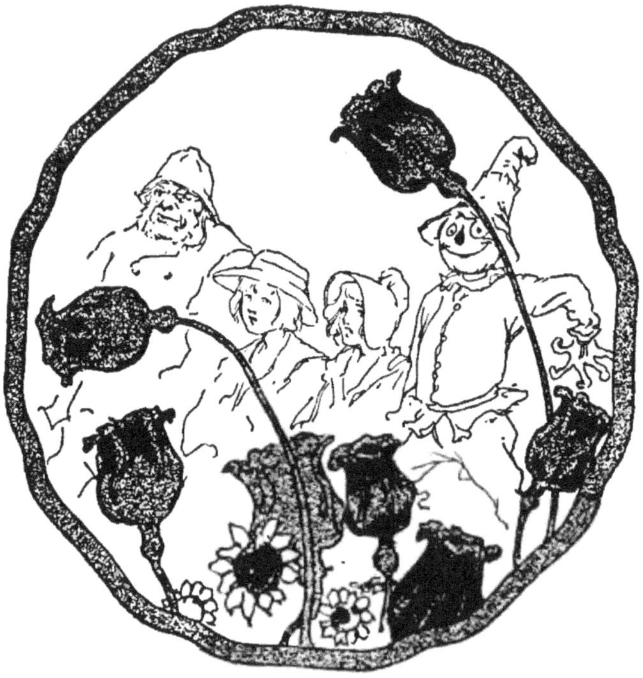

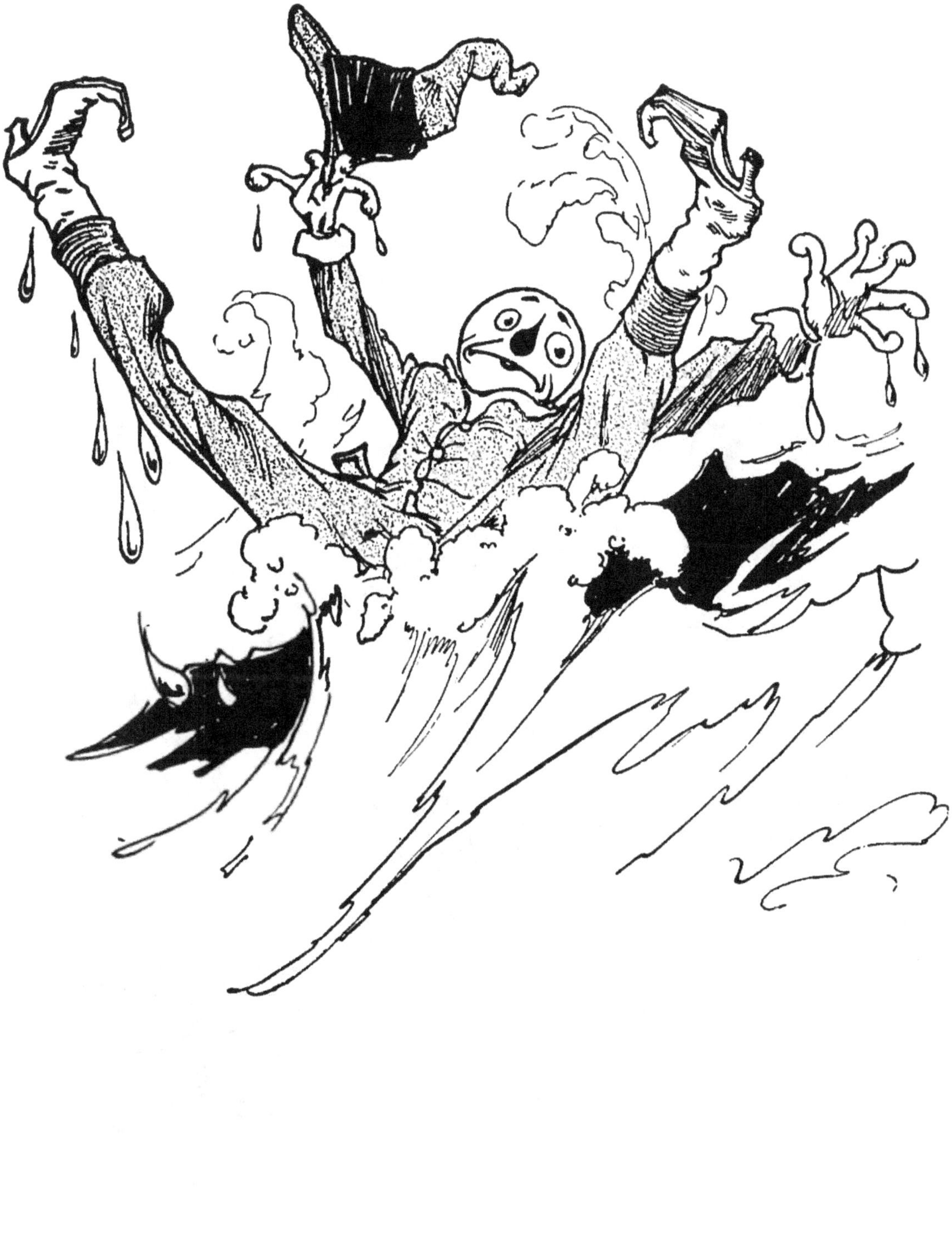

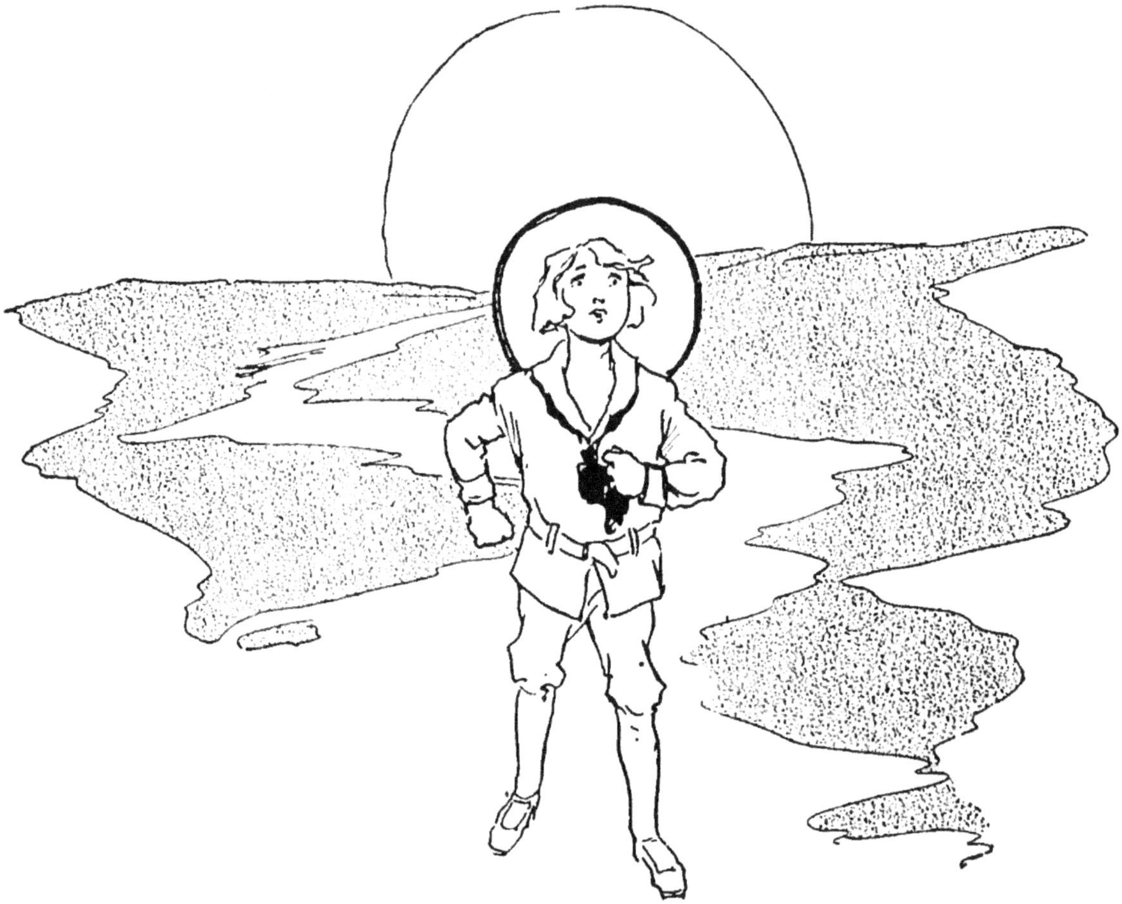

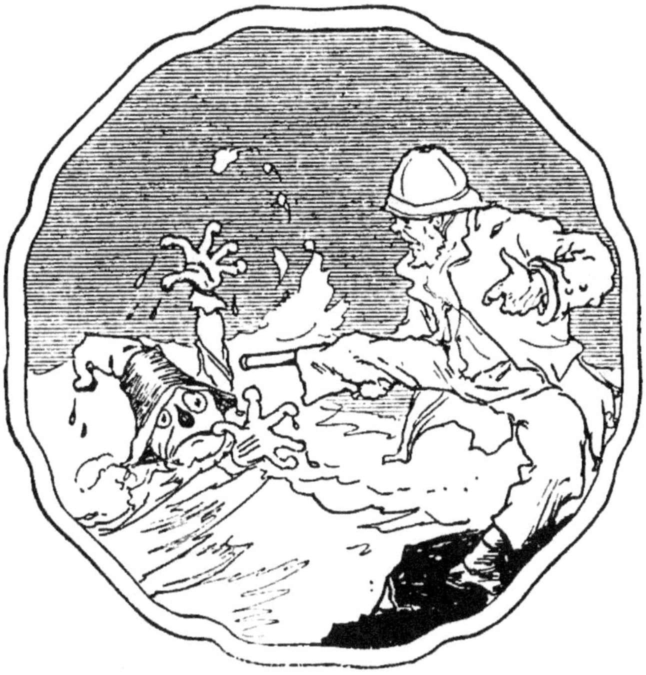

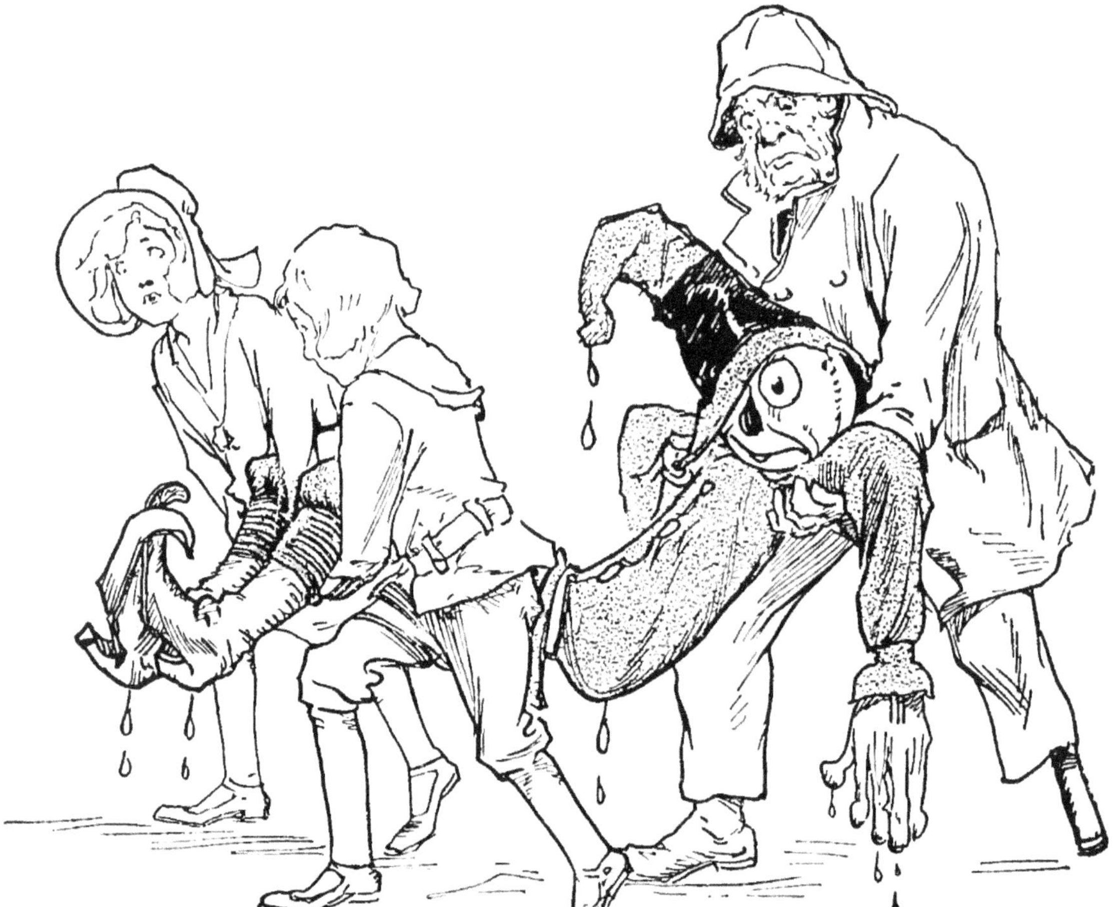

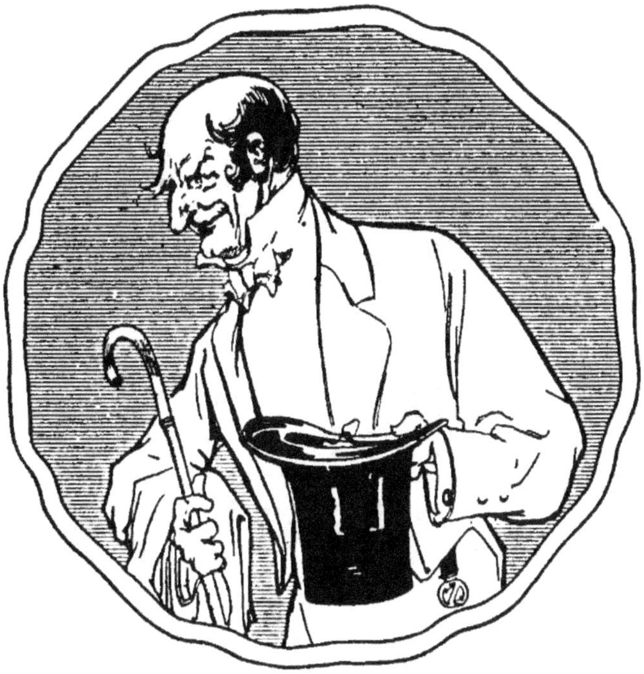

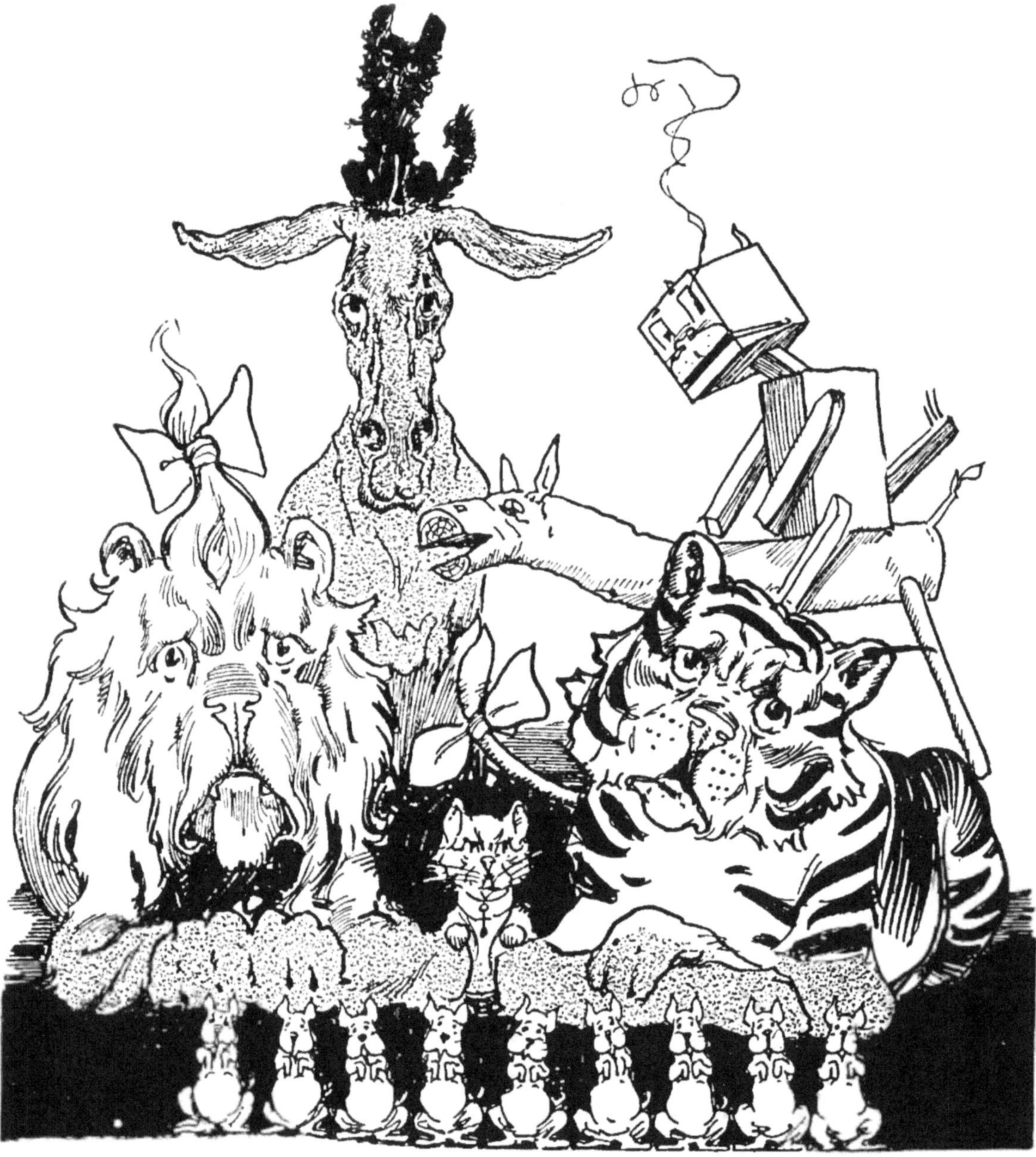

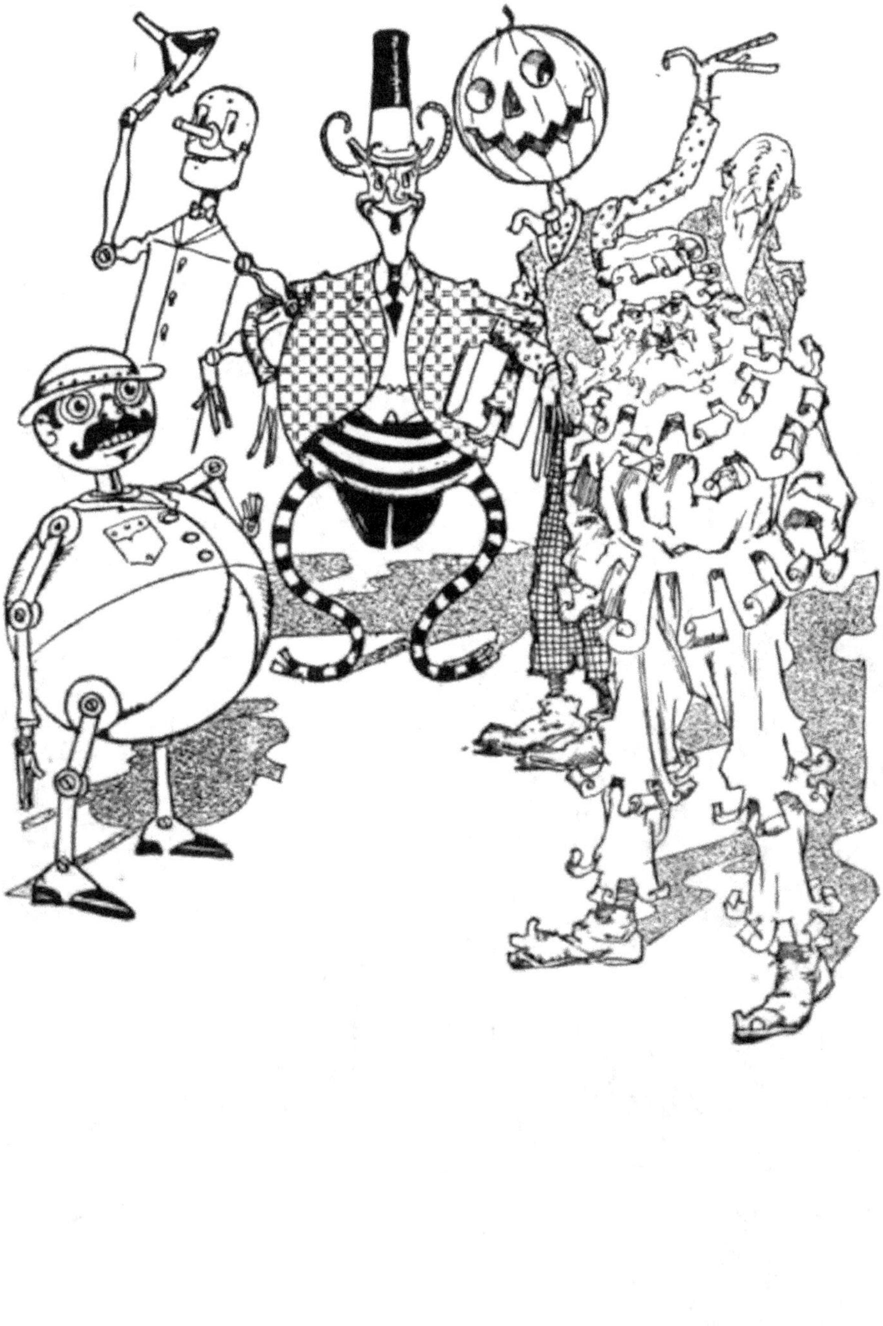

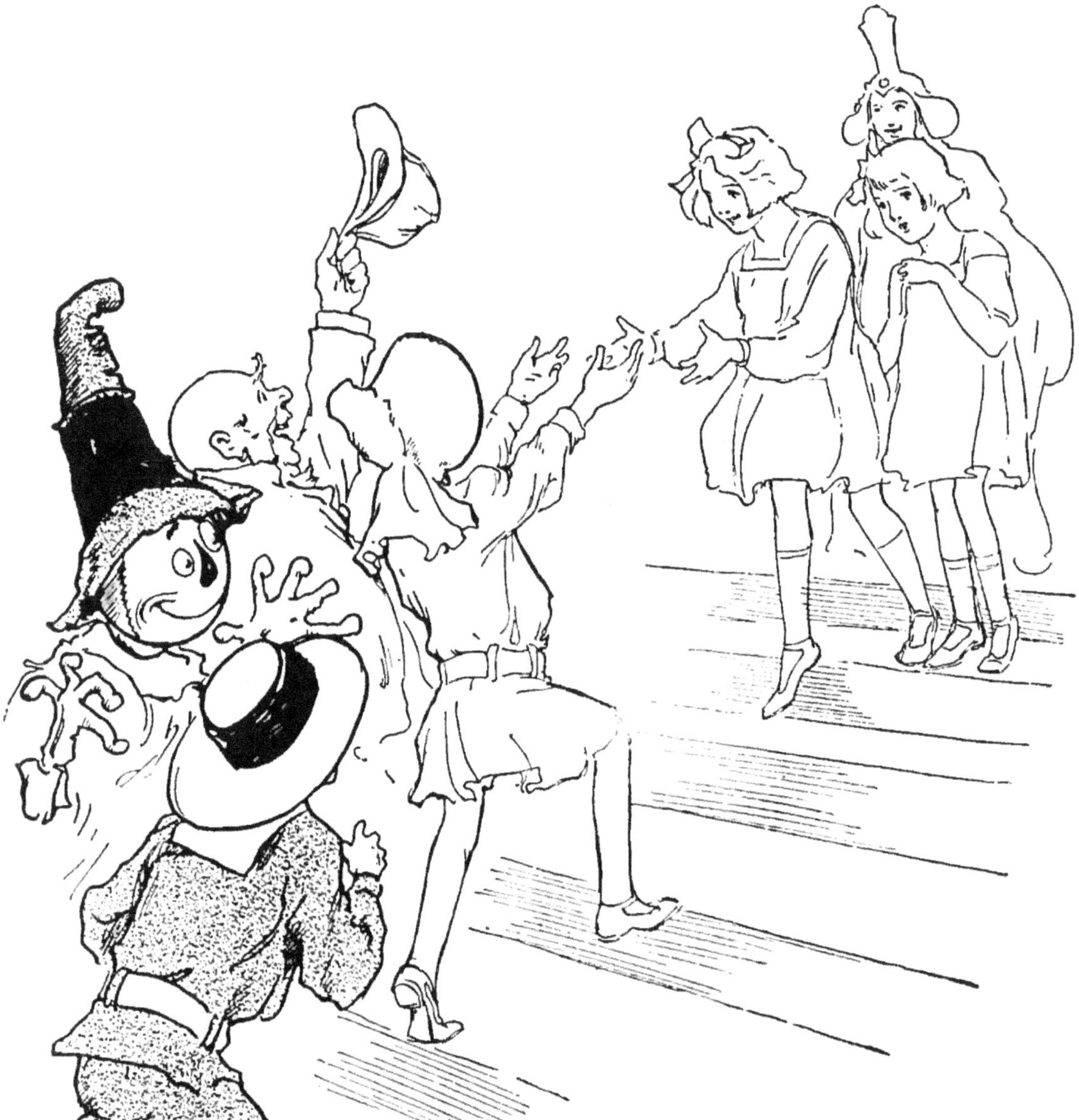

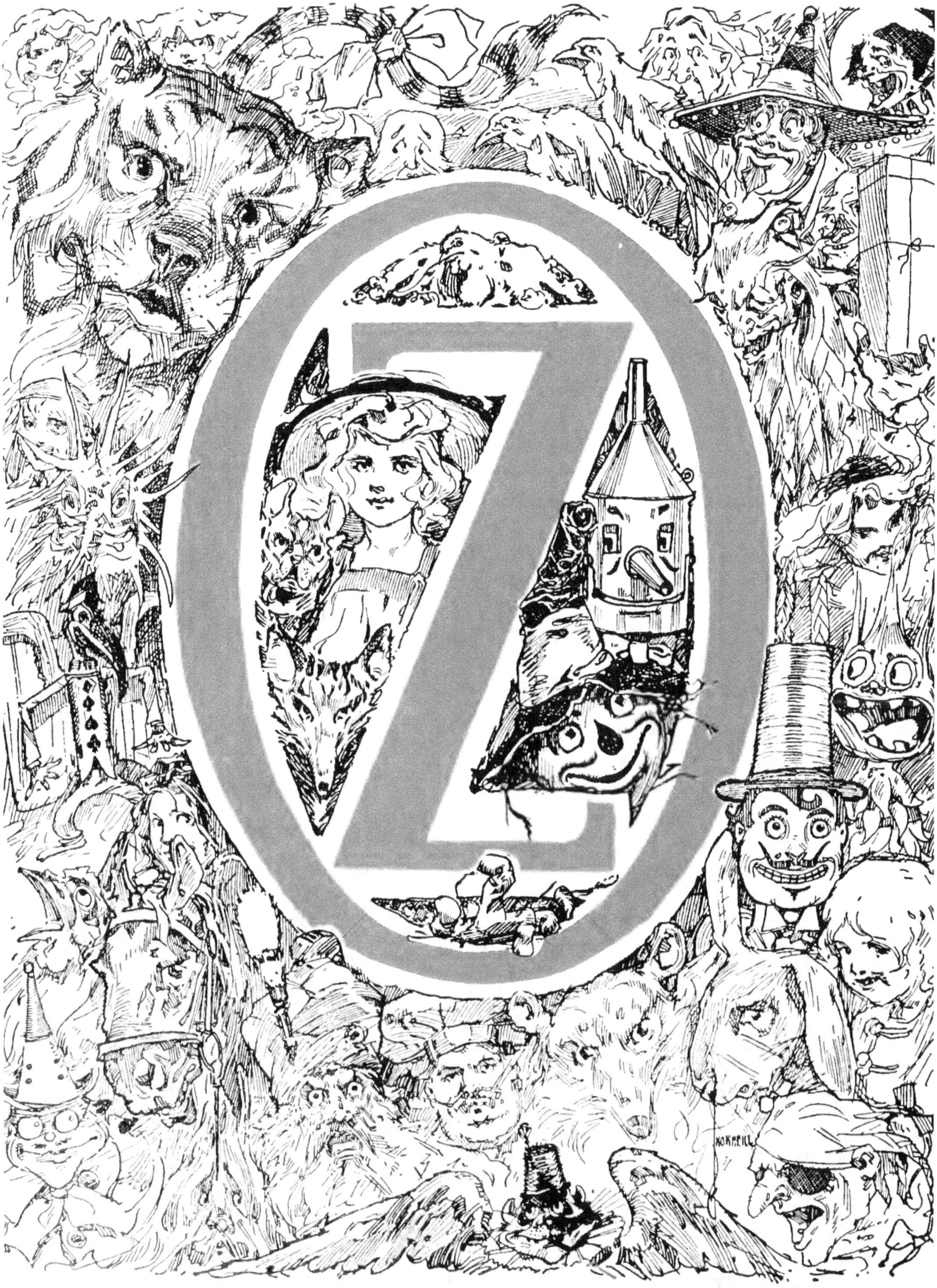
OZ

www.ingramcontent.com/pod-product-compliance
Lightning Source LLC
Chambersburg PA
CBHW081118180526
45170CB00008B/2894
9781546468127